Advance
The Digital Wrap

Impressive! Right on target! *The Digital Wrap* is an eye-opening, entertaining, and informative book that zeros in on customer-focused relationships using current technology tools and eMarketing concepts that many contractors have just plain missed. Contractors often keep up with technical advances in the industry, but most have not stayed current on customer service and marketing technology. *The Digital Wrap* guides contractors through current "best practices" for marketing in an age when everyone is seeking the attention of the customer.

— James Graening, CEO, B2B Sales Excellence

B2B customers are buying differently than ever before. They evaluate buying decisions based on confidence, perceived value, and ease of use. Giving the end user a phenomenal experience and keeping them engaged is more important than ever. *The Digital Wrap* reinforces the importance of user experience and embodies the new way of doing business. Billy will challenge you to rethink old strategies and to start working smarter. You will learn how to communicate with your customers online to give them an amazing experience that builds the value of your brand.

— Michael Crafton, CEO, Team 360 Services

Leaders looking to create a higher level of intimacy with their customers should read *The Digital Wrap*. This book has made us think differently about how we approach our customers, and incorporating some of Billy's key applications outlined inside have transformed our business model. He provides an innovative approach for driving companies into the digital world and making them indispensable to their customers. If you are looking for ideas to take your business to the next level, then read this book.

— Patrick Lynch, President and CEO, The Hiller Companies

The
Digital Wrap

Get Out of the Truck and Go Online to Own Your Customers

by Billy Marshall

with contributions from Bob Misita, Shawn Mims, and Jay Fiske

Contact the author at www.ServiceTrade.com

Thomas Noble Books
Wilmington, DE
www.thomasnoblebooks.com
ISBN: 978-0-9892357-3-0
Library of Congress Control Number: 2016903168
Printed in the United States of America
First Printing 2016
Cover design by 2FacedDesign.com
Editing by Gwen Hoffnagle

Table of Contents

INTRODUCTION

The DunnWell Story and the Origin of ServiceTrade

Have you heard the story about the terrorist plumber? Mark-1 Plumbing in Texas City, Texas, was flooded with phone calls when images of their service truck with two hooded thugs manning an anti-aircraft gun mounted in the back surfaced in jihadi promotional videos. Mark Oberholtzer, the owner of Mark-1 Plumbing, traded in his Ford F-250 for a newer model, but the truck wrap with the name of his company and his contact information was never removed from the old truck. After a series of auctions and relocations, the Mark-1 Plumbing truck landed in the hands of the Ansar al-Deen Front, a jihadist group operating near Aleppo, Syria. They mounted an anti-aircraft gun in the bed and used the truck in a series of propaganda videos. Anyone who wants to recall Mark-1 Plumbing can just search "terrorist plumber," and there is the phone number to give Mark a call.

Taking your brand online along with a good story can deliver extraordinary visibility for your business – just ask Mark Oberholtzer. When his truck wrap went online, people all over the world learned about Mark-1 Plumbing. Because you probably do not want to be remembered as the "terrorist plumber," your online story should instead tell a tale of terrific customer service. Your company becomes memorable and easy to recall when you build an online connection to your customers through your service activities. I call this concept the "digital wrap."

No doubt you are familiar with truck wraps. You probably have your logo, business name, and contact information on the side of your company trucks and vans. It's good, free advertising. It's foolproof as well because the truck wrap cannot be forgotten back

1

at the shop like a ladder or a special tool. No one has to remember anything or do any extra work for the truck wrap to leave positive impressions on prospective customers as the truck crisscrosses the service territory.

The drawback of a truck wrap, however, is that the impression is fleeting. Once your truck is out of sight, your brand is out of mind. The information never moves from short-term memory to long-term memory, and customers cannot easily recall your company when they need service. Outside of someone taking a photo of your truck with a smartphone and forwarding it along – or making a jihadi promotional video – your truck wrap cannot go digital or online.

What common service activities, like driving the truck in the service territory, could you take online to build customer impressions? What about scheduling notifications? Arrival check-ins? Or after-service reports with before and after photos? Or repair quotes with photos or video documenting the problem you are offering to fix? And service history on your website for customer self-service? And positive customer reviews? What if all of these were online so that it was easy for the customer to search, review, and recall your company when service was needed? What if every service call could potentially yield hundreds of online impressions? What if all the stuff in your filing cabinets was filed online? What if the information that is currently stored on computer hard drives in your office was instead stored on an Internet cloud so that the information was available to everyone all the time? And what if none of these online impressions required any extra or specialized work, just like the truck wrap – foolproof advertising with no extra work?

Taking your service activities online is how you build your digital wrap. When your service activities are digital and online, it is easy for the customer to do business with you, recall you for more business, tell a good story about you, and refer you to others. With a digital wrap, your company brand is always in the palm of your customer's hand – just an email or online search away on their smartphone. This book is all about helping you discover techniques for building a digital wrap – taking service activities online to connect to customers and maximize the value of your service brand.

I am not going to suggest that you tweet or blog or become a *search engine optimization* expert, because these techniques are not practical for you. Specialized marketing work that does not involve taking care of a customer will be ignored. Instead I'm going to show you ways that you can use the power of the Internet to continually market your business while simultaneously making your service calls more efficient and effective. If saving money on advertising and giving your technicians the potential to serve more customers each day sounds like something your business needs, this book is for you.

But before we go any further, you're probably wondering who I am and why you should pay any attention to *The Digital Wrap*. I discovered the power of a digital wrap thanks to a guy named Joe Dunn. I met Joe in February of 2010 at a Starbucks in Durham, North Carolina. It was seven in the morning – cold, dark, and raining – and I had nothing else on my calendar for the day. I'd been fired from a Silicon Valley start-up three months earlier after bickering with the CEO about how to run marketing and sales. Turns out being fired was a blessing because the Silicon Valley company tanked, and Joe was about to make me a terrific offer.

Joe blew into Starbucks and sat down to a hot black coffee and proceeded to tell me stories about his company, DunnWell. Honestly, I didn't understand most of what he was talking about – fire safety systems, kitchen exhaust cleaning, and national restaurant chains.

However, when Joe told me his company was growing 30–40% each year, my ears perked up. Then he told me DunnWell had no field technicians but instead used an Internet application for managing service delivery and engaging customers. Joe had my full attention now.

"Billy, we are growing like crazy because we have learned how to engage our customers online. Most companies we compete with are still operating in the dark ages. Customers often wonder if any service actually got delivered at all, or did they just receive an invoice for nothing? I want you to take what we have started and build a company that helps other service contractors use our online approach to grow."

I was intrigued with Joe's idea, but I was still skeptical. What were the odds that a service contracting entrepreneur had actually put together an application that would be interesting to the market and would scale? How could Joe have hired the talent to get an online software application right?

On the other hand, I had nothing better to do other than figure it out because I was unemployed. "Okay, Joe. Let me get some time with your tech guy, your customers, and your business partners to check out what you have. I'll also do some research into the market to see what others are doing." Joe said he would have all the meetings set for later that week. Could I accommodate that schedule? Sure. I was unemployed.

True to his word, I met several customers, some service partners, and Brian Smithwick, Joe's tech guy, before the week was out – Joe is not one to let grass grow under his feet. Turns out Joe had hired a superstar, because Brian was the real deal. He had attended the same high school for gifted science and math students as the CTO of my former company, who also happened to be the former CTO of technology titan Red Hat. Brian had also attended both Wake Forest and Texas A&M on scholarships – not too shabby. He built all of DunnWell's applications using the same scalable technology used by Amazon, Google, and Facebook.

When I met with DunnWell's customers and business partners, both groups raved about the capability of DunnWell's ServiceNet application. Here's what I heard:

- "Easiest company in the industry to work with because of ServiceNet," proclaimed the service partners.
- "All the information is organized and available anywhere I need it so that we can be more productive delivering service."

- "Before ServiceNet, I never really knew if anyone had actually cleaned the exhaust system ductwork. DunnWell shows me before and after pictures online," one restaurant facility leader commented.

- "Now we require all vendors to use photos because of DunnWell. Unfortunately, most of them are not very good at it. The photos arrive in email or even on CDs instead of being posted online for easy reference. What a drag. DunnWell makes it so much easier to view things online."

Finally, when I reviewed the other applications in the market for service contractors, I saw that there was nothing to help users tackle the problem of bringing customer service online. All the applications for service contractors were focused on internal operations, and none were designed to engage customers. As best I could tell from a quick review, the market was wide open for an application company to help service contractors take their service activities online.

I happily agreed to join Joe at DunnWell to help Brian and the rest of the team. After approximately two and a half years we had doubled DunnWell's revenue – a reflection of the strong value customers place on working with a company that uses technology to manage service and provide online information.

Cintas purchased DunnWell's service business in September of 2012. We formed a new company called ServiceTrade based upon the technology from DunnWell, and we began offering our customer engagement platform to service contractors in April of 2013. As of April 2016, we have over 250 service contractors using our applications to manage service delivery and engage their customers online.

If you are a service contractor, I hope this book motivates you to create your own digital wrap for engaging your customers and prospects online. Like a truck wrap, the digital wrap delivers marketing impressions simply by delivering service.

I believe technology is going to drive extraordinary changes in service contracting. Engaging your customers online will be essential as technology changes your market. The first several chapters of *The Digital Wrap* show you the pending competitive pressures you will be facing and gives you strategies to survive and thrive. You'll discover what happened in other industries and how you can use those lessons to win big in your market.

Next you'll read a series of guideposts and practical solutions that will help you increase the value of your business by creating a digital wrap. You will learn how to:

- Turn your dispatch notifications, equipment history, repair quotes, and after-service reports into valuable online customer impressions

- Use Internet reviews to take control of your online reputation in order to attract new prospects without being extorted for advertising fees by digital toll collectors

- Make simple and inexpensive changes to your website that will also help maximize the value of your online presence

- Evaluate software and technology quickly and wisely without any requirement for specialized technical knowledge

Best of all, I won't ask you to do something that is not already natural or familiar. Sure, you will need to change a few things, such as using the Internet instead of the telephone for customer engagement – which is what your customer wants anyway! A few simple changes to your processes and technology can create mountains of online content that sticks your brand in the mind of your customers and builds memorable impressions with prospects in the digital neighborhood.

If you are ready to attract more customers and make the customers you have today even happier with your service, you will benefit from a digital wrap. Let's get started designing yours now.

Billy Marshall
Durham, North Carolina
March, 2016

CHAPTER 1

From Amazon to Aardvark: The Parallel Universe of Service Contracting

Software is eating the world.
— Marc Andreessen in *The Wall Street Journal*

Imagine a universe parallel to the one that we live in today. In this parallel universe, Amazon is not the king of online commerce. Instead a company called Aardvark leads the way. Aardvark specializes in service, not retail. Unlike Amazon, Aardvark is not named after one of the wonders of the world, the rich ecosystem of the Amazon River that sustains an incredibly diverse population of wildlife. Instead, Aardvark is named after an obscure burrowing animal of Africa because any name that begins with AA is listed first in the Yellow Pages. Similar to Amazon, Aardvark has a website, but that is where the similarities end.

At aardvarkservice.net you can browse for services that you might want to purchase. You must call Aardvark, however, and speak to someone to learn how much a service costs and when they might deliver it to you. If you call when everyone is busy or after business hours, you will speak with an answering service. They will take a message and promise that someone will get back to you shortly. Sometimes they do, and sometimes they don't. Aardvark is funny that way. If you reach Aardvark and decide to buy a service after your phone conversation, you can expect a follow-up call at a later time to confirm details on delivery.

Aardvark service delivery is typically quick and courteous during business hours because Aardvark really does value your business.

Often the follow-up call actually comes from the service tech when he is en route to your business or your residence. Sure enough, you spot the shiny Aardvark truck with the Aardvark logo and the catchy slogan on the side – *"We Dig Deep to Make You Happy."* Products sold and delivered by Aardvark are often hard to see and appreciate, however, because the product is service. Service is usually delivered to the roof or the attic, or perhaps the crawlspace, the utility room, the elevator shaft, or inside the ductwork. Often the only way you know that service was delivered at all is because you saw the Aardvark truck in the parking lot.

Sometimes the service tech leaves behind an invoice. It is typically handwritten on a piece of paper with the Aardvark logo on it. Sometimes you can read the handwriting, and sometimes you cannot. Maybe the service tech explains what was delivered, but the information on the invoice is usually just some cryptic accounting codes with vague descriptions and perhaps the prices you agreed to pay. Sometimes the invoice is wrinkled, with coffee stains, and occasionally some cigarette ash. Every now and again there is a smear of ketchup and the scent of fries wafting from the invoice. You promptly throw away the invoice when the driver leaves.

Aardvark is also different from Amazon in other important ways. Whether you like the service or not, there is no place on the Aardvark website to leave feedback so others can benefit from your experience. You can go to other websites to leave feedback and read reviews about Aardvark, but this is a pain. The folks who go to that trouble usually have only nasty things to say about Aardvark. Most of that feedback is not really helpful.

Unlike Amazon, the Aardvark website does not recommend any complementary services for you. Sometimes the service tech insists that you will not be happy with your purchase unless you buy a complementary or upgraded service because the one you selected from the website is cheap. The service tech might also insist that he discovered other problems that you cannot see when he delivered your service to the roof, or the crawl space, or the attic. If you believe what he is telling you, and if you really like him, you might buy new products he offers from the truck to replace your faulty ones. Most likely you do not.

While Aardvark currently dominates the market in this parallel universe, for some reason they never seem to grow the way Amazon grows every year. Unlike Amazon, many customers do not buy from Aardvark more than once. Some do, of course, because they really like the Aardvark service tech and they think he is honest and hardworking. Most customers, however, are not excited about doing business with Aardvark. The truck is shiny, the logo is pretty, and the slogan is catchy, but the experience of doing business with Aardvark is just not rewarding or memorable.

This parallel universe is not an imaginary universe; it is the current state of service contracting. It is real, and we are all living in it today parallel to the same universe where Amazon dominates retail commerce. Few, if any, of the innovations pioneered by Amazon and other online retailers have made their way to service contracting. Aardvark still rules the service contracting landscape, and this silly comparison of Aardvark to Amazon illustrates how vulnerable service contracting companies are to the threat of disruption by an Amazon-like force.

The real irony, and perhaps the biggest threat to Aardvark, is that Amazon does not even produce or deliver most of the products they sell. Amazon does not have delivery drivers or delivery trucks with their logo and a catchy slogan on the side. Amazon has very little control over the physical products they sell; Aardvark has complete control over the service the customer receives. Yet customers return again and again to purchase products from Amazon. Why is that? How is it that the most valuable retailer on the planet has no retail outlets? As you will learn in a later chapter, Uber, the most valuable transportation company on the planet, owns no vehicles. What are these companies doing differently to be so valuable to their customers?

Amazon and Uber are drastically different businesses, but they are alike in that both use technology to deliver an amazing customer experience. They provide rich information and total customer service convenience through online interfaces. Customers enjoy buying online from Amazon and Uber. They find both to be fast and easy without requiring a single phone call for customer service. Features such as reviews, photos, and complementary products help Amazon customers feel like savvy consumers who are making smart buying decisions. Uber shows driver information, fare estimates, online driver reviews, and real-time information on the location of the driver. Customers trust Amazon and Uber to deliver superior customer service.

The tremendous success of Amazon and Uber is a huge threat to service contractors. Amazon, Uber, and others have proven that **you do not have to actually produce and deliver products to own the customer.** The customer gravitates to the BEST SERVICE EXPERIENCE independent of who actually delivers the service or provides the labor.

Imagine what would happen if Amazon went into the service business and all of the Aardvark service technicians one day decided that they wanted to work with Amazon instead of Aardvark? What if the Aardvark customers began to buy from Amazon, with the same technicians managing the delivery of the product? The pretty Aardvark logo and the catchy slogan would not be in the parking lot, but the customers would get photos of the product, online delivery notices, website reviews, purchase history through an online account, complementary service recommendations, comparative price-shopping – all with absolute convenience, transparency, and no phone calls. Aardvark tries hard, but Amazon is easy. If Amazon entered the service business, all the Aardvark customers would quickly become Amazon customers.

The parallel worlds of Amazon and Aardvark are colliding. The Aardvark trucks are shiny and the slogan is catchy, but the Amazon experience is more convenient and more memorable because online impressions are easy to engage, store, recall, review, and reengage. Maybe the customer will remember the Aardvark logo and the slogan, but it is more likely they will search the web or their inbox for the latest offer from someone else. The customer is definitely going to trash the handwritten Aardvark invoice. How can Aardvark be memorable and important to the customer when the truck wrap is fleeting and the invoice is in the garbage?

The quote at the beginning of this chapter comes from a *Wall Street Journal* editorial written by Marc Andreessen back in 2011. Marc is an investor in many high-technology companies including LinkedIn, Facebook, and Twitter. He is also a board member at Hewlett Packard, and he was a founder of the company that kicked off the Internet revolution, Netscape. When he says "software is eating the world," he means that the power of software applications coupled with the Internet and cheap mobile devices is going to disrupt *every* industry. Amazon used technology to disrupt local retailers. Netflix used technology to disrupt Blockbuster and even the cable companies. Google used technology to disrupt the advertising world. *The Digital Wrap* later explores how Uber is disrupting the taxi companies and how Tesla is disrupting Ford. Your service contracting business is going to be disrupted by technology as well.

(If you want to read the full article by Marc, search for "Andreessen software eating the world" in your favorite search engine.)

Digital wrap is the term I use to describe technology applications that can help you provide a memorable buying and service experience for your customers. Like the ubiquitous truck wrap – every service contractor has one – the digital wrap will become a brand expectation for services. Customers simply will not remember service contractors who do not have a digital wrap. Would you send your technicians out to deliver service in dirty, rusted-out trucks with hand-stenciled logos on the side? Yet every day they probably leave behind handwritten, coffee-stained, carbon-copy "tickets." Is this the impression you want to leave with your customer? Is this the way you want to be remembered? The digital wrap is a way for you to use technology to become memorable to your customers before someone else uses technology to take them away from you.

My goal with this comparison of a fictitious Aardvark service company to Amazon is to give you a little jolt of reality. I want you to be motivated to make changes *before* your business comes under threat from technology-savvy, online competitors. If you are already feeling the threat from new-age competition, I want to heighten your sense of urgency for building your digital wrap.

In the next chapter I move from the fictitious example of Aardvark to real examples of new competitive scenarios that are emerging today in service contracting. You will definitely recognize at least a few of them, and others are lurking just around the corner. Tons of capital is flowing into technology companies that have an eye on your customers and your profits. If a fictional Aardvark is not motivating, perhaps the hard numbers behind capital investment in new Internet-enabled service contracting competitors will be.

CHAPTER 2

Avoid Internet Connection Tolls: Build Your Own Customer Connections

The purpose of business is to create and keep a customer.
— Peter Drucker

Right now someone is using the Internet to build a digital connection to your customer. The purpose of this connection is to become a trusted purveyor of information and services related to your trade expertise. The emerging competitor is technology-savvy, and they have a ton of capital backing their efforts. Their plan is to charge you, and every other service contractor as well, a toll each time the customer requires your services.

Your toll collector might be a national service company that sells a contract to a headquarters office for locations you currently serve directly. They will use a network of local providers just like you to deliver service and contribute information to their online application – an application that documents the service and provides a rich repository of analytical data for the customer. You might continue to serve nearby locations, but it will be at a 25–30% discount on your current fees for identical services. You will also pay an administrative toll associated with the extra "paperwork" to update their "third-party" application that manages the service data – a treasure-trove of rich information designed to keep them connected to the customer forever and keep you locked out.

Maybe the Internet toll collector in your business is a manufacturer selling "smart" equipment with Internet connections that help them plan and manage equipment maintenance and repair. The manufacturer sells a three-year extended warranty, and the Internet connection helps them deliver "smart service" based on the operating parameters of the equipment. Because you never established a connection to the customer to demonstrate your value as the expert for this type of equipment, you were not invited to the table when negotiations about equipment purchasing and service plans were underway. You will take a 30% haircut on your service calls going forward because the manufacturer controls the customer relationship along with the service data. Your company will become the labor driving the trucks and turning the wrenches, and you will probably also hold the parts inventory to meet the service-level agreement promised by the manufacturer.

If you do residential work, your toll collector might be Yelp or Angie's List, both of whom are watching your lead-generation activity on their site. When they decide you need to pay more to reach customers in your service area, you will get a call from a highly skilled sales representative. "If you don't pay more, poor reviews might begin to populate your profile, slowing down your business and forcing you to increase your advertising and discounts to attract customers," proclaims the sophisticated technology sales rep. "What poor reviews?" you ask. "The ones I just wrote," replies the hungry wolf without the slightest note of remorse for his extortionist business practices. (Don't believe it? Search for the movie *Billion Dollar Bully*.)

Maybe the Google Nest thermostat is going to start monitoring the HVAC equipment that you currently service, and the notification of a compressor malfunction will be a lead that Google sells to the high bidder… and you never even knew there was a problem at your former customer.

Do these scenarios seem imminent or feel familiar? Have you experienced these challenges in your business already? Do you believe these examples are anomalies that will disappear, or do you believe these trends are here to stay? Consider these facts:

Porch, an Internet start-up founded in 2012, has raised nearly $100 million in funding from venture capitalists. Their mission, according to their Crunchbase profile, is "to change the world one home at a time by making home improvement easy for homeowners. The Porch marketplace spans all 250 home improvement, maintenance, and repair categories."

Amazon launched its Amazon Home Services in November of 2014. Amazon is huge, and booked revenue of over $100 billion in 2015. They do not enter new markets that have only modest upside; they look for new opportunities that can deliver billions of revenue to their top line – otherwise it is not worth the effort. Service contracting is an area in which they plan to siphon off their fair share from customers who cannot locate a trustworthy service contractor on their own.

Google paid $3.2 billion in cash for Nest, an HVAC thermostat and smoke detector company, in February of 2014. This deal is *not* about thermostats, but instead it is about monitoring the customer's environment in order to make purchase recommendations. Think about that statement and the amount of money Google paid for a company with estimated revenue of $200 million. How would you like to get a 15X multiple on your revenue as the value of your company?

These facts are evidence that the service contracting market is a rich target of profit potential that is ripe for harvest by the Internet titans. In the last chapter I introduced you to Marc Andreessen and his famous quote that "software is eating the world." The examples above are real evidence that Marc is right. In fact, Marc is an investor in Pro.com, another online home-services company, through his venture capital firm Andreessen Horowitz. Jeff Bezos, the founder and CEO of Amazon, is also an investor in Pro.com. Marc, Jeff, Google, Angie, Yelp, and Amazon would not be after this market if it did not represent a future bonanza for their shareholders.

Nothing about these new investments or the new service players makes them evil or illicit – with the notable exception of the extortion scheme highlighted above and practiced by some of the Internet review brokers (you know who they are). All these new actors in the service contracting space have shareholders who expect them to deploy their capital, skills, and technology resources in areas in which they reasonably believe they will create an above-average return on investment. The service contracting market, with an estimated annual commerce value well in excess of $300 billion in the US and Canada alone, and with rich gross margins in the range of 35–60%, represents an untilled field of profit potential to cultivate and harvest. The fact that their "fair share" will come at the expense of the existing market incumbents (that is, you) is of no concern to them or their shareholders. As the Peter Drucker quote at the beginning of this chapter reminds us, the purpose of business is to "create and keep a customer" in order to generate shareholder returns. If taking the customer from you is easy because you have not protected that customer with a memorable online customer service capability, so much the better for them.

Now, are you ready for a really good joke? While Amazon and Google and Marc and Jeff might be the face of new competition, they are also your salvation. Not that I believe the best brands will work as the truck depot and labor bureau for these guys and their new companies – far from it. I expect that the labor pool for these guys will be small one- or two-man operations that do not take on the task of building a brand or a digital wrap. Larger service companies have too much overhead to make a reasonable profit after the third-party toll collectors skim their "fair share" off the top. The joke is that Amazon and Google (as well as Apple and others), through their investments in cloud computing and technology like Android and iPhone, will become your allies in building your digital wrap. In subsequent chapters I provide a great deal of detail on how this all came about, but let me give just a few examples here:

In the case of Amazon, they have built an extraordinary cloud computing business called Amazon Web Services. In less than 10 years, AWS has gone from zero to over $8 billion (yes, with a B) in annual revenue. ServiceTrade, and thousands of other software-as-a-service (SaaS) companies, use AWS as a high-performing, low-cost infrastructure for applications that we sell to companies like yours. With the information technology expense that a single service contracting company might have incurred for running an online application 10 years ago, ServiceTrade can support thousands of companies (yes, thousands). You can pay a fraction of the cost from 10 years ago while ServiceTrade still has plenty of profit because of Amazon. You also get to avoid all of the information technology muck associated with servers and storage and operating systems. Thank you, Jeff Bezos!

In the case of Google, technology like their Maps application and Android make it possible to deliver information from the technician to the customer (and the office) regarding service delivery so that everyone feels informed about status and value. GPS data, photos, audio, and video are available to practically everyone in real time for the small cost of an annual data plan with your carrier. What is even funnier about Google is that their search algorithm prioritizes local content over other related content. What this means is that if you are aggressive in generating local content in your service area that you post to your website, you can use Google as your advertising engine without ever paying them anything for ad words! Yes, you read that last sentence correctly. If you do your digital wrap properly, you will pay Google far less than you would for ad words and get much more traffic from their search engine. And they arm you to compete with their ad words with online content you generate from their Android phones!

Aardvark was a silly, fictitious example to draw a contrast between service contracting and other industries. The threats revealed in this chapter, however, are real, and they are aimed squarely at your service contracting business. Equally real and available to your business today is the means to fight back. I bet you have already deployed smartphones and tablets to all of your technicians. I am also willing to bet, however, that you not are using these new tools to engage the customer as much as you are to update accounting information back in the office. Am I right? Is it all about a signed invoice or a credit card swipe, or is it about a better customer experience?

Think about the common thread in all of the threat scenarios above. **They all revolve around data the customer uses to make thoughtful decisions about spending money on services.** The national service companies have data that demonstrate trends and accountability. The contractor review sites have data and photo imagery that demonstrate consistent quality of service. Amazon has data related to complementary products and services (a TV *and* the service to mount it to the wall) plus reviews, service schedules, and comparative pricing. Google knows the performance of the HVAC system and who is qualified to address pending failures. Are you collecting data like these to help your customer make a decision for your services? Probably not. But that is okay because I am going to show you how. *And* you have likely already invested in most of the tooling to do it. But first you have to refocus your data priorities on customer experience instead of on your internal accounting requirements.

In the next chapter I tell the story of Uber in order to further cement the importance of customer experience over internal operating efficiency as the number one technology priority for a service company. Uber has become the most valuable transportation company in the world in less than eight years, AND THEY DO NOT OWN ANY CARS! Instead they own the customer experience. Read on to see how they did it and learn some more key lessons for your success.

CHAPTER 3

Don't Get Ubered: Focus on the Customer Experience Instead of on Your Internal Operations

Ubered – verb – to kick the crap out of something using a computer. To beat someone in any game without them barely having a chance at winning.
— from the online Urban Dictionary

If you were to eavesdrop on a management meeting at a taxi company back in 2010, you probably would have overheard a series of questions about improving operating efficiency:

- "How can we increase profits relative to each driver payroll hour?"
- "How can we have less idle time and spend less on fuel?"
- "How can we have fewer dispatchers for each fare revenue dollar?"
- "Should we be investing in electric or hybrid vehicles to lower fuel expense?"
- "What can we do to lower the cost of vehicle maintenance and repairs?"

Meanwhile, the folks at Uber in San Francisco were asking these questions instead:

- "How can we create the absolute best customer experience for a taxi ride?"

- "What hassles can we eliminate using technology in order to create an amazing and highly differentiated service?"

- "How can we use this new technology experience to attract customers that we keep forever?"

Today, a mere six years later, Uber is an enterprise worth over $80 billion – a higher value than all of the other taxi and car service companies in the world combined. The tragic mistake the taxi companies made during their 2010 planning meetings was to assume that their service was a protected local commodity. They did not even consider trying to create a premium customer experience. Instead they focused their management attention on internal operating efficiencies that were largely irrelevant to the customer. Are you making the same assumptions and mistakes about your market and your business today?

Uber, by contrast, focused on the customer and how technology could be used to enhance the customer's experience. They made it easy to hail a cab with a mobile phone. Uber's phone app shows the location of the driver and the type of vehicle, connects the rider with the driver via text or call to coordinate pickup, and eliminates the aggravation of exchanging the fare upon completion of the ride. They empower the customer after the ride by always requesting a review of the driver and the experience. The Uber service is sometimes cheaper, but also sometimes more expensive than a typical taxi ride. And it is WILDLY popular. Uber won – in a landslide and in the blink of an eye. Now taxi companies are fighting for Uber's leftover profit scraps. Turns out that internal operating efficiencies are irrelevant when all of the customers choose the vendor with the superior service.

Many service contractors are making the same mistake the taxi companies made six years ago. They are focusing all of their management resources on trimming small amounts of incremental fat around the edges of their operational "chuck steak" instead of transitioning their capabilities into the market for "bacon-wrapped filet mignon." There is nothing wrong with trimming fat (or chuck steak for that matter), *if* there is a zero probability that a game-changing disruptive force will enter the market. If the competitive landscape is absolutely static, and will remain so forever, trim away at the fat, serve up the chuck steak, and ignore the potential for creating a better product and a differentiated customer experience.

I firmly believe that the chuck-steak-type service is going to become unpalatable to a market that craves bacon-wrapped filet mignon – especially when filet mignon service is available at the price you are asking for chuck steak. A competitor delivering an amazing customer experience through technology will emerge for every trade in almost every market, and all the customers will flock to that provider. Focusing all your management efforts and technology decisions on improving internal accounting operations leads to a perfectly irrelevant process for zero customers.

So how can you avoid getting Ubered by a competitor? One approach to defend against the inevitable disruption from the Internet is to appeal to government. That is what the taxi companies in France are doing in response to being Ubered. They are burning tires in the streets and striking with demands that the government intercede on their behalf. This defense might work for a short time in France and other socialist societies, but it is unlikely to work in economies that embrace capitalism.

In New York City, taxi companies are now responding to Uber by investing in the development of their own Uber-like experience for the customer. After a well-capitalized technology-savvy competitor wiped away their profits, they are now pooling their resources to copy the capability of Uber. If they ever actually get the new technology-enabled service to market, it is pretty likely that Uber will have moved forward yet again. Uber will continue to improve their customer experience in order to remain firmly entrenched as the premium service provider. The old-school taxi companies will continue to fight for the scraps at the low-margin end of the service spectrum.

The best way to avoid being Ubered is to Uber everyone else in your market. Customers will always pay a premium for a service that is free from hassles, uncertainty, and risk. Some of the innovations in customer service might be simple changes in process, but the truly remarkable changes that transform industries and set the best competitors apart from the field are driven by technology.

Consider the case of DunnWell, the service contracting company that preceded ServiceTrade. Joe Dunn observed that his customers hated the hassle, risk, and uncertainty associated with service companies that clean the grease from the exhaust ductwork of a restaurant. It is messy and invasive to deploy a pressure washer to the roof and spray chemicals and hot, pressurized water down into the restaurant through the ducts. For the vendors that do it correctly, a job well done comes at a pretty high price. The customer, however, cannot see what has been accomplished other than through the aggravation of water on the floor, hood filters in the sink, and possibly an inoperable fan motor that shorted out during the cleaning. Restaurant owners rarely (never) go up on the roof and lift the fans and peer down the ducts to see what was accomplished. They just feel the aggravation of the after-service foul-ups.

Joe's solution to the problem was to show customers photos taken by the crew so that they could easily review the quality of the exhaust cleaning service. By using an Internet application to display before and after photos of both the ductwork and the condition of the kitchen, a bond of trust and appreciation was established between the cleaning crew, DunnWell, and the customer. The customer could easily see the value and quality of the service provided, which eliminated risk and uncertainty. With this simple technology innovation, DunnWell was able to grow very quickly because of the unsatisfied demand in the market for a hassle-free (or at least lower hassle) approach to a very invasive and messy service. Today the entire market for kitchen exhaust cleaning services is defined by the ability to engage the customer online with digital photos that prove the value of the service.

It is impossible to predict exactly which innovation in each service trade and across every market will lead to extraordinary outcomes for the savvy practitioner. However, there are some basic principles and common themes that always lead to enhanced results:

Right now – Customers want immediate information regarding the status of their service. They don't want to wait for a dispatcher to call a technician, get an update, then call the customer back with a translation. The taxi experience with Uber is a perfect example: Uber shows the customer the exact location of the driver and the type of car, and connects them directly with the driver in real time. Find ways to give your customer accurate information when they want it, which is right now.

Show me don't tell me – Customers do not want the watered-down, Reader's-Digest version of the story, but it is time-consuming and very expensive for a technician to write down everything they observe. They simply will not do it. It is much better to show the customer the problem – in living color. Photos and video are a great way to draw the customer into the experience. DunnWell changed an entire industry with photo validation of kitchen exhaust cleaning. Uber shows the driver location on an interactive map. Images and graphics are much more powerful representations of information than a text-based summary.

Digital accounts – No one likes filing paperwork and organizing information, so don't make your customers do the administrative work for your service records. If you become the digital filing cabinet for these records, they can access and review them any time with zero hassles. Your website becomes the gateway to information and value, making your service "stickier" and enabling you to charge a premium. All modern customer service systems offer this capability: Amazon and eBay with purchase history; your bank with online banking; Orbitz with trip history; Uber with online payment and receipts. When you create a history of your customer's service work, they have a reason to return to your website to view that history – and then to contact you for their future needs.

Online reviews – Asking the customer for feedback and posting that feedback for the world to see is very empowering for the customer. It is also a check on bad behavior for the service worker. If everyone understands that the customer has power, including the customer, a balance of power is achieved between the expertise of the service company and the review privilege of the customer. Reviews are powerful attractors for prospective customers as well. Think about how online retailers use them. Think about how you value them for online purchases in your personal life. Embrace online reviews as a mechanism for enhancing customer service and attracting new customers.

Price transparency – Understanding the fair value for a purchase helps close the sale with the customer. When they have doubts about value, they hesitate. Note how Amazon indicates the price range for items from all sellers on their site. Uber gives an accurate estimate of the fare *before* you hail the driver. If you are the service company that helps the customer understand fair value, they will trust you. You do not have to be the low-cost provider, simply the fair, high-value provider. Price transparency builds trust.

Proactive service – Using data to establish service schedules and deliver proactive services that prevent equipment failures and avoid service interruptions is the pinnacle of thoughtful customer service. After demonstrating an ability to predict the future by offering repair advice *prior* to a breakdown that ultimately occurs (if the customer ignores the advice), the value of your services increases immeasurably. Service fees become much less important than the predictability of reliable equipment. People will pay a premium to avoid expensive equipment failures.

Any trade service professional will tell you that skilled labor is not the driver of value and profit in service contracting. Expertise, trust, and superior customer service play a critical role in building an enduring, premium-profit relationship with valuable customers. Digital service records that demonstrate expertise and facilitate collaboration with the customer eliminate risk and hassles, which in turn leads to long-term, high-profit relationships. It changes the competitive dynamic in a market in which most service contractors are simply responding to service calls for malfunctioning equipment. **Getting paid for what you know is much more lucrative than getting paid for where you go.**

Great customer service is ultimately defined by online collaboration between the service contractor and the customer. The lesson of Uber is clear. Show the customer your value online so that YOU are the company using computers to "kick the crap" out of your competition instead of being on the other side of that beating.

Uber is a great example of how a new competitor became the dominant force in a service industry by using technology. The customer-experience lessons from this disruption show clear customer service strategies for improvements that service contractors can embrace. In the next chapter I tell the story of another young but high-flying company, Tesla, and demonstrate how manufacturers are going to connect to your customers and pinch your profits. These manufacturers may be your partners today, and they may be your partners tomorrow, but only if you are prepared to use their tactics and negotiate with them from a position of strength.

CHAPTER 4

Rise of the Machines: The Tesla Lesson for Service Contractors

Your clothes: give them to me. Now!
— Arnold Schwarzenegger in *The Terminator*

Tesla is the hottest car company on the planet today. Just in case you are not familiar with them, Tesla sells only very high-end, high-performance electric vehicles. While you may have heard of Tesla, there are three things you might not know about the company that can directly influence your business. Intrigued?

- Tesla has no dealers. They sell directly to customers.
- Tesla performs all the maintenance and repair services on the vehicles they sell.
- Tesla's market value is extremely high relative to other car companies.

Let's start with that high market value and then examine how the other two unique aspects of Tesla's business might be contributing to their high share price. The current market value of Tesla is $33 billion – a pretty impressive valuation for a company that is only about 13 years old. Ford, by comparison, has a market value of about $57 billion, and they are 100 years older than Tesla. For every dollar of annual car sales, Tesla generates $18 in shareholder value. This factor is known as a revenue-to-value multiple. It is generally used for fast-growing companies that are not yet profitable in lieu of the more common price-to-earnings ratio (or P/E ratio).

The higher the revenue-to-value multiple for any company, generally the more effective that company is at attracting and keeping valuable customers. How much stock price value is generated for every revenue dollar? A company does not have to be profitable to be valuable to its shareholders when it is rapidly growing sales to an attractive customer base. To compare Tesla to Ford once again, Tesla has an 18 multiple of revenue to value, and Ford's revenue-to-value multiple is 0.4. This is not a typo – Tesla's revenue generates 45 times more shareholder value than Ford's revenue.

So why is Tesla more than 45 times more valuable than Ford relative to each dollar of car sales? Shareholders believe the Tesla business model has much more potential than the Ford business model. It is tempting to believe that the difference is all about electric vehicles and the relative value of these in a world of finite fossil fuel resources. No doubt this future growth dynamic plays a role in Tesla's sky-high valuation. Interestingly, however, Tesla's share price is not tightly correlated to the price of oil.

Figure 1 – Price Appreciation Comparison of TSLA and OIL, the iPath S&P GSCI Crude Oil ETN, from January 2013 through January 2016.

Maybe it is Tesla's overall business model as a customer- and technology-focused manufacturing company. Let's start with the way Tesla sells its vehicles. They establish a direct connection with the customer via their very modest albeit high-tech showrooms, which only display a couple of example vehicles. Because vehicles are essentially manufactured to order, there is no need for large showrooms to hold dealer inventory. In contrast to their diminutive showrooms, Tesla has a very rich web presence to engage prospects, create excitement about the product, and guide the customer through the purchasing process.

Augmenting Tesla's official online marketing are Tesla customers and enthusiasts who often create interesting media features that ultimately promote the Tesla product. For example, Brooks Weisblat, of the website DragTimes, created a video about people's reactions to the Tesla "insane" mode acceleration. This hilarious video has been viewed over six million times. This type of buzz from consumers creates conversations and viral marketing. People are excited about Tesla cars. When was the last time you were so excited about a product that you were motivated to make a video about it?

(If you are interested in seeing Weisblat's video, you can find it by typing "Tesla insane mode video" into your favorite search engine. Warning: it contains explicit language.)

All automotive companies rely on racy or relevant user experiences to promote their products – trucks battling each other in mud pulls, race event coverage, etc. You'll see logos and other promotional images prominently displayed at events for car lovers. Tesla, however, has taken direct customer engagement to a level far beyond advertising and brand promotion. By eliminating the dealer distribution model and engaging directly with prospective customers, Tesla is a new kind of car company with a fresh and engaging approach.

After the car sale, Tesla maintains that direct relationship with the customer for service. Tesla provides customers with a mobile app for engaging certain features of the vehicle (like remote start to warm or cool the cabin) and for receiving notifications from Tesla regarding updates and service scheduling. Each vehicle has a seventeen-inch touchscreen display for direct communication between Tesla and the customer regarding software updates as well as for managing certain settings and features of the car. The vehicle also includes a mobile network, so it is always connected to the Internet, which means that Tesla can monitor information about vehicle performance and determine if any service or upgrades are required.

For non-scheduled repairs, or if a malfunction occurs, it is possible that Tesla can fix the vehicle via the Internet. If not, the customer is notified by email and through notifications in the mobile app, and Tesla meets the customer with a loaner and transports the car to the repair center. In this way, Tesla anticipates the need for service and provides an experience that is free from risk and hassle for the customer. Additionally, Tesla is always in touch with the customer and the product through "over the air" updates and upgrades to the car's digital operating system. Tesla's treatment of their customers is the very definition of the online customer service model that I believe will become the standard for all products and services.

> *The best way to experience service is, of course,*
> *not to experience service.*
> — Elon Musk, CEO, Tesla

With this statement Musk insinuates that "service," as historically defined, is an inconvenience for the customer. Musk goes on to elaborate that smart machines should almost never need any service, independent of whether the user has read the manual or not. The product should, in effect, be idiot-proof, particularly when connected to the Internet and subject to performance monitoring and remote updates by the manufacturer.

(You can find and read the full post about service philosophy by Elon Musk by searching: "Elon Musk Best Service and Warranty.")

As with Uber and the taxi drivers in France, some auto-dealer groups did not like Tesla's approach. They saw the danger of losing customers to a new Internet-driven service model, and they appealed to the government to save them from Tesla's direct, online customer service approach. In New Jersey, Michigan, Texas, and a few other states where the car-dealer lobby is very strong, Tesla was initially banned from selling its cars at company-owned stores. The ban, however, was more ludicrous theater than a real impediment, because customers can easily buy a Tesla and arrange delivery via the Internet. And the ban did not prevent service from being delivered by Tesla service centers in these states. It was simply a lame attempt to slow down the inevitable competition brought about by the Internet and new, streamlined business models.

Even with the unique performance attributes of their electric vehicles, it is unlikely that Tesla could have succeeded as they have without the Internet as a means to connect with customers for both sales and service – too many entrenched interests would have been operating against them. Online customer engagement coupled with a proactive, data-driven service model enabled Tesla to succeed against much larger competitors and local market interests like the dealers.

Do you imagine the folks at Ford and at every other manufacturer in the world are paying attention to the Tesla story? You can bet that they want their companies to have shareholder valuations that approach those achieved by Tesla. You can bet that other car companies, and all equipment manufacturers for that matter, are looking to duplicate Tesla's preventative maintenance systems and extended warranties. Are you seeing more equipment come standard with a display touchscreen and a mobile network built into the system? Think about it. Every customer would love the equipment manufacturer to guarantee performance over the equipment ownership lifecycle. Who wouldn't want that experience? If possible, customers just want equipment to work without hassles or service of any type.

Before the Internet, the logistics and costs of direct sales and service made it impossible for manufacturers to consider this model. Instead they relied on networks of distributors and dealers to deliver customer service. Those same distributors and dealers might continue to service the customer in the future, but be assured that the savvy manufacturer is considering ways to establish a tighter relationship with the customer after the sale. The Internet will be the conduit for the manufacturer to engage this new business model. They will sell a service contract at the time of purchase, connect the equipment to the Internet to manage service, assemble a network of servicers for any required onsite visits, and use the Internet as the conduit for all communication and coordination. This will help them lower costs and improve outcomes. What does it mean for you, the service contractor? If you are an equipment dealer in addition to being a service contractor, should you be concerned about the Tesla lesson?

The question for the service contractor is whether to keep your clothes or hand them over to the Terminator. Are you going to own your customers or simply become the truck depot and the labor bureau for the manufacturer and accept a 20% pay cut? The labor portion of any service work is worth at best 80% of the value the customer is paying for service (recall the Uber example where the driver gets 80%). In many cases it is worth less. Labor can be eliminated completely in cases where the customer does self-service based on online guidance in the form of video sessions (think FaceTime and related cameras) or how-to videos on YouTube. If you do nothing, you could end up losing more than your shirt to the manufacturers – the Terminator will take your pants and underwear, too.

Or you can make another choice. You can continue to be "the expert" and help your customers achieve higher performance at a lower cost throughout the equipment ownership lifecycle. To do this, you will need to use all the same tactics as the manufacturer – sell service contracts, offer equipment warranties, connect the equipment to the Internet, collect operating data about the equipment, assemble a network of servicers including yourself, and use the Internet as the communication conduit in order to lower costs and improve outcomes. Everyone is scrambling to attract and retain the interest of the customer. The only way to survive and thrive is to be the expert who is MORE connected with MORE data so that you become MORE relevant to the customer.

I believe there are two unique, but related, strategies for preparing your business for the inevitable encroachment of the manufacturer onto your turf. The first strategy is broadening the scope of your company's expertise. Aim to encompass as broad a range of equipment and manufacturers as possible. Digging deeper into various equipment performance specifications – both published and practical field experiences – will help you be the neutral third-party expert for your customer. Collecting data across your customer base regarding the performance of the equipment arms you with valuable information for helping customers make thoughtful purchasing decisions. Determining which non-OEM parts are actually identical to the OEM parts (built on the same assembly line, in fact) helps you provide customers with valuable information while providing you with higher profits. Use information to cement your brand as the trusted expert.

There are a hundred ways to use information to become more valuable to the customer and build a more profitable business once you declare that your allegiance lies squarely with the customer and their outcomes. None of these, however, resembles storing records in a filing cabinet. You have to find ways to take this information online to build a collaborative approach that encompasses all of your employees, partners, and customers.

Your second strategy is to develop independent monitoring expertise. If the equipment is going to be connected to the Internet, why shouldn't the data come back to you? There are a couple of key operating attributes for most types of equipment that can be monitored to predict an imminent failure and related business interruptions. Some examples are current, temperature, pressure, vibration, voltage, humidity, and cycle time. The wise service provider can lock into a few of these monitoring opportunities across a handful of equipment types to position themselves to provide tremendous value to the customer. Chapter 12, "Smart Services, Monitoring, and the Internet of Things," explores this idea in detail.

Most customer equipment does not resemble a Tesla automobile – a large-scale and integrated value proposition. Instead most customers have numerous types of equipment from numerous manufacturers, and each one has a unique signature to be monitored for performance. Connecting multiple types of equipment to the Internet and offering a monitoring solution is an opportunity for you to be more valuable to the customer. The single interface they trust for managing their equipment and its performance is you and your company!

Tesla is demonstrating how to build an incredible business by establishing a direct connection to valuable customers. Their tactics, however, are not limited to manufacturers; they apply to your service contracting business, too. In fact, most service customers probably prefer that you help them with their equipment maintenance because you are local, but only if you can also eliminate the hassles of service through better connections. Give customers choices about the equipment they purchase with all the benefits of the best smart service programs offered by the manufacturers from a single provider – YOU. Eliminate the hassles and risk of operating that equipment with smart-service capabilities that protect the customer from failure risks and poor performance.

Your digital wrap needs to include every type of service connection you can build to the customer *and* to their equipment. If you can become the trusted expert for every equipment purchase, your profit margins will not depend on things like emergency service labor rates – service which, by the way, sucks for the customer – but instead on maintenance and monitoring fees. However, the predictable nature of better outcomes for the customer should allow your margin to move up while hassles for both you and the customer move down. **And eliminating hassle and improving outcomes is what you are aiming to achieve with your customer experience.**

The Tesla lesson demonstrates how connected equipment drives value through increased communication, fewer hassles, and less risk for the customer. In the next chapter we examine how online advertising and review sites attract customer attention and extract digital tolls. You can use the tactics of these online sites, however, to hold the interest of your customers and attract new customers as well. You can, and should, create and own your online reputation as part of your digital wrap strategy.

CHAPTER 5

Digital Tolls:
The Only Rule Is There Are
No Rules

If you're not paying for it... you're the product being sold.
— blue_beetle on MetaFilter

How did Google become the most valuable company in the world? Google sells advertising, yet no one would confuse them with the Yellow Pages. Google became valuable because they organized most of the information on the Internet in a way that consumers find useful. Google uses computer algorithms to make judgments on the value of Internet content, and those algorithms are so effective that consumers trust Google to provide the best results for their searches. Because consumers trust them, Google is in a privileged position to help customers make purchase decisions – and take their fair share of the transaction.

There are other information companies that also collect and organize information online similar to Google, such as Bing, MSN, and Yahoo. And, most important for you as a service provider, there are online advertising companies that focus on local businesses. I'm sure you have heard of Angie's List, Yelp, Porch, Pro.com, HomeAdvisor, Thumbtack, and several others. Also like Google, the primary business model for these companies is advertising, although some are increasingly taking a cut on the business transactions initiated with their applications. It is important to understand at a high level how all of these platforms work and make judgments on how, or if, you are going to participate in their commerce model.

To explain online advertising platforms, I invited Bob Misita, the CEO of LeadsNearby, to write the rest of this chapter on the rules, or lack thereof, associated with these platforms. LeadsNearby is a web marketing agency devoted exclusively to service contracting marketing. Bob is an expert on how to use online applications for your benefit.

As a service contractor, what do you own? Your trucks? Equipment? Maybe your building? You likely own or control most of those pieces, but who owns your customer relationships? What about your online brand and reputation? Do you own and control these?

Your online brand and reputation, as well as your customer relationships, are very real and important elements of your business value that you can manage and optimize. Fortunately there are many things you can do to maximize the value of your online brand and reputation if you understand the game. Play the game correctly and you will increase your Internet traffic without large expenses from Internet advertising tolls.

You've probably driven on a toll road or bridge. That's a helpful metaphor for understanding the business model of online advertisers like Porch, Yelp, Angie's List, and others. These sites collect Internet user traffic through the creation and curation of Internet content. Then they charge you, the business owner, tolls to direct some of that traffic to your website or phone number. As the quote at the beginning of this chapter indicates, the user traffic on these sites is the product that is being sold to you, the advertiser.

However this toll road metaphor is actually backwards, because it is usually the traveler who pays a toll to use a road instead of the road owner paying a toll to receive the traveler. On the Internet, you, the business owner, pay the toll to the website that directs the traffic to your company. The important part to remember is that the toll collector needs *both* traffic *and* destinations for the model to work. Understanding how they generate traffic and how to make your destination (that is, your website) attractive helps you minimize the tolls you pay for receiving travelers. The most attractive websites pay the smallest tolls for traffic. Make sense?

Let's review the rules that these digital advertising properties follow. But wait… there are no rules! Each of these websites has total control over how information is displayed on their site and apps. The only real rule they have is to maximize the size and quantity of the tolls that you, the advertiser, pay to them. To do this they focus on increasing traffic and maintaining trust with consumers who visit their sites. High traffic and high trust yield higher toll volume and higher toll prices for you to pay.

These toll collectors use business profiles along with customer reviews for those profiles to attract Internet travelers. Business profiles are descriptions of businesses like yours. The profile reviews provide helpful information that potential customers use to make purchasing decisions. A profile for your business, along with reviews and other information, can exist on each of these online platforms WHETHER OR NOT YOU CREATED IT OR MANAGE IT. This is an important point because you want to at least be certain your profile is accurate *and* you want to be responsive to bad reviews. Just because you are ignoring your profile and reviews on these sites doesn't mean that your customers and prospects are ignoring them.

Let's use Yelp as an example so that you can see how this all works. Yelp has a simple yet aggressive business model. Yelp's content revolves almost entirely around customer reviews. These reviews attract Internet travelers because reviews help the travelers make decisions about what businesses to patronize. Yelp's revenue is driven by advertising tolls charged to the owners of profiles who want the first listing in a review search.

Yelp calls this pay-to-be-first status the "featured" status. Becoming "featured" allows you to include higher-quality content on your profile, which improves the quality and popularity of your profile. Low-quality, non-featured profiles are not helpful to Yelp because they do not drive advertising tolls – travelers do not pay tolls for roads with bumps and potholes that lead to low-quality destinations. Both Yelp and the owners of the low-quality profiles are incented to drive those profiles up in quality. If you pay Yelp advertising tolls, your profile quality increases – they will pave your road and smooth the potholes for you. If you have a high-quality "featured" profile and you stop paying Yelp, the profile quality falls, along with the traffic, until you reinstate the advertising tolls. Yelp raises and lowers the quality of the profile by determining which reviews are presented to the viewer. Yelp calls this selective display of reviews "filtering." There is significant speculation that when you pay, the bad reviews are "filtered" out so that the profile quality rises. If you do not pay enough, bad reviews are not "filtered" out until you pay more. Yelp makes the rules.

Yelp disputes claims that they influence reviews to drive toll revenue upward. They claim that paying an advertising toll simply assures the removal of competitive ads from your profile page. However, the sheer volume of claims by business owners to the contrary, the obvious financial incentive to behave otherwise, and the lack of transparency of the proprietary filters that govern what reviews are displayed (versus those that are hidden) leads a sensible person to conclude otherwise. The bad behavior is so blatant and obvious that Yelp's antagonistic practices toward advertisers are the subject of a feature-length movie, *Billion Dollar Bully*. The movie documents case after case of Yelp filtering reviews to maximize advertising tolls levied on profile owners.

All of the advertising platforms ultimately want to emulate the success of Yelp, so most follow Yelp's practices to some extent. So how can you coexist with these platforms whose interests are clearly not aligned with yours, or better still, thrive on their existence without paying crazy tolls?

The answer is pretty simple. Any traveler they direct to you, whether you choose to pay or not, needs to arrive at your destination, your website, and never leave. You need to use the toll platforms to increase the visibility of your website while using the value of reviews for your own benefit. Once a customer experiences your brand value, they never again need to return to the toll collector to find another service company.

It is important that you begin by registering or "claiming" your profile with each of the advertising toll platforms whose travelers seem like your customers. Profile registration creates pointers or roadmaps to your destinations – your website on your domain and your primary business phone number. In order for these roadmaps to be useful, they must ALL ALIGN AND POINT IN THE SAME DIRECTION. In other words you cannot have different roadmaps on different platforms. The description of your business – the phone number, the web address, the physical address, the value proposition for customers – MUST ALL BE EXACTLY IDENTICAL on each platform.

When all the roadmaps to your destination point in the same direction, Google and Bing notice this alignment and reinforce the flow of traffic. You will see your site climb the search rankings when all profiles are aligned. This is a good thing.

Next, pay attention to poor reviews and address them online and, ideally, with the disgruntled customer. Ignoring poor reviews is a bad strategy. It makes it seem like you do not care about the poor service. Ideally you will resolve the complaint in a manner that leads the reviewer to post a positive review about your attentiveness to their issue. When you receive an alert for a review that is not positive, follow the alert back to the review site and enter a sincere response with an offer to correct the situation. If the customer is a sincere individual, this approach often enables you to make the proverbial lemonade from a poor-review lemon. If the customer is simply a troll looking for a cut-rate price, at least you have demonstrated that you pay attention to customer concerns, and other traffic on the site will see that attentiveness.

However, it is not enough to just point traffic to your website and react to bad reviews. You also have to offer travelers the same amenities available to them at the toll site. Toll sites offer review information to qualify and support purchase decisions. High-quality, sincere reviews of your services on *your* website help customers make purchase decisions also, *and* this review content makes your site more attractive and important to search engines.

Toll site reviews also offer the customer an outlet to express their satisfaction, or lack thereof, with your service. The ability to post their own review, or to somehow reach you with feedback, is empowering to the customer. Both ServiceTrade and LeadsNearby offer a review tool that makes your site more valuable to customers. Details about how to use reviews to attract travelers to your website are covered in chapter 8, "The Basic Formula for an Effective Service Contracting Website."

Using reviews as both a mechanism to help prospective customers make a purchase decision and as a feedback loop for service-quality monitoring makes your brand stand out on the Internet. When coupled with memorable customer service as discussed throughout this book, the customer has no need to ever return to the toll site to find a service contractor they can trust. They have you. Information and engagement empower customers and build trust, and you get to own them forever. That's how you win the game with the Internet toll collectors and win more revenues for your business.

Below is a list of some of the online platforms where you can "claim" or create your profile to generate a roadmap/pointer back to your website. I have ordered them from highest priority to lowest. Not all of these are perfect for your business, so you should do a small amount of homework on each one to ensure your customers are using these sites to find service contractors like you. I provide a short description of each to help you get started. You can delegate these profile registrations to your web agency, but just be certain to follow up behind them and ask explicitly for a listing of the "citations" they have created for you.

Google My Business

Launched first as Google Places, then renamed Google Plus, this was Google's not-so-successful attempt to compete with social media entities such as Facebook and Twitter. Today it is simply an extension of Google's search platform. If you want Google to display your website in any search results, it is IMPERATIVE that you have a business profile on Google My Business.

Google sees your website first through the lens of information that you register with Google My Business. The profile you build on Google My Business MUST BE EXACTLY IDENTICAL to the information on your web page. If you work with a marketing agency, they may want you to use a different phone number on some of these sites so they can measure the impact of their marketing. Don't be persuaded to follow this marketing advice, because it confuses Google search results.

Set up the Google My Business profile yourself – do not trust it to an agency unless they give you administrative access. If you fire the agency, you want to keep the trust and authority that you have built up through the profile instead of starting again. Setup is not difficult or time-consuming. Just search the phrase "google my business" and click the "Get on Google" button.

Social Media Platforms

Your customers are communicating with each other and exchanging recommendations socially on Facebook, Twitter, LinkedIn, and Instagram. You should create a profile on each of these or have someone do it for you. Each of these is worthy of setting up the profile page. It is easy and free, and it increases your Internet traffic. (An entire chapter is dedicated to LinkedIn later in the book.)

Yelp

Despite the challenges documented above, you should still claim your Yelp profile. You're likely going to have a Yelp profile for your business whether or not you create and manage it, so it is better to own it and control it. If you do not claim it, you cannot respond to negative reviews that are posted. Even if you cannot own the content posted about your company, at least you can respond. Registering with Yelp also gives search engines more directions to your website, which is a good thing. Remember to keep everything consistent, especially your website URL and telephone number.

Angie's List

Just like Yelp, you are likely to have an Angie's List profile regardless of whether you create and maintain it. Be proactive, claim your profile, and make it consistent with all others.

But even owning your Angie's List profile may not be enough to get Angie's List users to your profile page. Angie's List's big claim is that no contractor can pay to be on Angie's List; you simply set up a free profile for your business and people will find you. For a few select categories of service providers that might be true, because there are so few that all must be displayed for Angie's List to have any value whatsoever to the Internet traveler. For less-populated areas of the country where there are very few service providers, this statement also holds true. But what if you are an air conditioning repair company in Atlanta, Georgia? It's a safe bet that you will be paying Angie if you expect her to display your profile to potential customers.

It may be a wise move to advertise your business on Angie's List so long as the advertising provides value – meaning paying customers – and you can afford the cost. But it's important to know the terms. The bottom line is that when you sign a contract with Angie's List, make sure you can afford the expense, especially if the faucet of leads that they promise never turns on.

Directories

Directory sites are the modern-day version of Yellow Pages advertising. As with Yelp and Angie's List, it is important that you set up a consistent profile on the following sites:

YP
Kudzu
Dex
SuperPages
CitySearch
Manta

It only takes a few minutes to register with each of them, and the pointer back to your website helps elevate you in organic search results from Google, Bing, and others.

Pay-Per-Lead Platforms

Paid lead programs such as Home Advisor (formerly Service Magic), Porch, Thumbtack, Amazon Services, Google Home Services, and Angie's List Snapfix may be viable avenues for extending your brand. Definitely sign up for their free profiles, but be careful of the lead quality and the cost of leads from these vendors.

You can always hire an agency or assign someone in your office to perform these profile registrations. However, it is really important that you follow and understand these basic principles so that you are not misled or overcharged for the work. You should also definitely check behind the work to be certain it has been completed and you are getting the results you desire. These strategy tips minimize your digital tolls and maximize the traffic you attract and keep with your online brand and reputation.

CHAPTER 6

Lessons and Gifts from Retail and Consumer Technology

If I have seen further it is by standing on the shoulders of giants.
— Sir Isaac Newton

Since the late 1990s, the retail commerce industry has been completely reshaped by the Internet. Brands like Amazon and eBay deliver retail commerce based on online shopping interfaces and their expertise in processing information. They present rich information and online engagement features that help the customer make an informed buying decision. For the items that do not sell in large volumes, an army of niche retailers uses the very same platforms as their sales channel, filling in product gaps with their unique items.

The result is that customers can shop, compare, and select almost any merchant item online with high confidence. Consumers believe that they are getting a fair value, and they experience extraordinary customer service via their online accounts. Shipping notices, purchase history, recommendations, reviews, return instructions – in short any information relevant to customer service – are delivered online and without telephone calls. No one even thinks to call Amazon or eBay. I am not certain I would even know how or what number to dial. Old brands such as Borders, Circuit City, Blockbuster, and Radio Shack did not adapt to this new online reality, and they have been marginalized or have simply disappeared.

Twenty years after the beginning of the online retail revolution, new brands are emerging on the Internet with a focus on reshaping the market for trade services. Angie's List and HomeAdvisor are household names. Brands like Porch, Pro.com, Facility Source, and others are emerging with new business models that rely on information, connectivity, and expertise – not local service presence. The monster Internet brands such as Amazon and Google are also getting into the services game. Amazon announced a new service known as Amazon Local Service. Google has purchased HomeJoy and Nest, while simultaneously revamping their search routines to allow them to skim extra margin off service searches through "qualified" contractors that are registered with Google. As with the online retail boom, some of these new ventures and innovations will be successful and others will fail in spectacular fashion. What is crystal clear, however, is that the rules for customer engagement and success are changing for service contracting just as they changed for retail.

I believe there are some key lessons from the transformation of the retail market that predict the future shape of the trade services market:

1. New Internet brands will emerge that emphasize information, expertise, and customer service without any requirement, or expectation from the customer, of local service capacity. The same trend dominated retail with no expectation on the part of the customer that Amazon or eBay open local storefronts.

2. An army of individual freelance laborers will fill the local labor capacity requirements of the Internet brands at a small markup on the prevailing labor wage. Note how many products on Amazon are actually sold by Amazon versus one of their affiliated partners. eBay operates exclusively on a freelance model.

3. High-volume service purchases (water heater replacements, HVAC preventative maintenance, burner start-up) will experience extreme price pressure as transparency and online comparison shopping replace the race to the driveway. Both Amazon and Walmart used information technology, albeit in different ways, to drive brutal efficiencies in distribution

for the most commonly purchased items (TVs, cameras, electronics, books, music, etc.).

4. Existing service businesses that do not adopt technology to gain an edge in customer service and build customer loyalty will become marginalized or disappear.

As gloomy as these predictions might feel, there is positive news for service contractors from the Internet retail revolution. The massive technology infrastructure spending that characterized the buildup of the Internet retail titans actually benefits your efforts to go online to engage your customers. Progressive service brands can implement extraordinary capability for online customer service with very small incremental monthly expenditures.

The old model of purchasing expensive servers, software, and consulting for information infrastructure is being wiped away by low-cost software-as-a-service (SaaS) and cloud computing models where everyone shares in the expense of the infrastructure. Amazon has actually emerged as the largest purveyor of low-cost cloud infrastructure. They offer infrastructure on a pay-as-you-go subscription model that most software providers, including ServiceTrade, are utilizing to deliver applications to their customers – at a fraction of the capital costs that were formerly required. This new low-cost, easy-to-adopt model for application capability is one of the important "gifts" from the retail revolution.

I am regularly asked by ServiceTrade's prospective customers about the fees for photo storage. Many of ServiceTrade's customers record as many as 40 or more photos for each service job to illustrate the value delivered to the customer. They are incredulous when I tell them that they can take as many photos as they like and there will not be any storage surcharges from ServiceTrade. Photo storage is not an extra charge because ServiceTrade uses Amazon's Simple Storage Service (S3) for redundant, secure storage of more than eight million photos and work documents. Amazon charges ServiceTrade less than $50 per month for S3 storage of these eight-million-plus files. Charging customers extra for storage is not even a thought because it is practically free to ServiceTrade anyway.

Perhaps even more important than the massive infrastructure that resulted from the transformation of retail commerce are the extraordinary innovations in the personal consumer technology space. Innovations from Apple, Google, Samsung, and others are a boon to the service contractor who is looking to generate content and make connections to customers. Massive consumer spending on technology enables gargantuan research and development budgets for these companies and their products. Apple alone spends over $8 billion annually on R&D – much of it for technology that is extraordinarily beneficial in your pursuit of rich online connections to your customers.

This trend of consumer innovations leading to business innovations is called the *consumerization* of business information technology. You can search "consumerization of IT" online and you will find all manner of commentary and research indicating that consumer trends are dominating the technology adoption agenda for business information technology professionals.

Consider this example of consumer technology driving business capability: An Apple iPhone 5S is currently available for no extra cost when purchasing a $30 to $40 monthly data plan. The phone includes an eight megapixel camera, an audio recorder, a 1080p HD video recorder, GPS, and map applications. Imagine the array of equipment technicians would have carried along to a job just five years ago to replicate all of this capability. As a bonus, all this technology in the phone is connected to the Internet to enable potentially seamless collaboration between the technician, the office, and the customer. With the right applications, huge amounts of administrative labor formerly associated with creating, processing, and distributing digital service records (GPS info, photos, audio, video, reports) just disappear.

Consider also *geolocation* – another of the gifts from the consumer Internet revolution that can be used commercially. Google offers a commercial map application to technology companies like ServiceTrade via a set of *application programming interfaces* (APIs – more on those later). All manner of location information is now available to ServiceTrade customers because of the power of Google. Map projections of pending jobs can be used to optimize technician work routes. When entering customer information into ServiceTrade, after a couple of key strokes on the name and address, Google "guesses" what you are typing and suggests the detailed location information. Nine times out of ten it is correct, and office staff can simply select that Google location record to be their record. Instead of typing in an average of two hundred key strokes to enter a customer record (no doubt with a mistake or two), less than twenty key strokes are required to get an accurate record. ServiceTrade pays Google for this capability, but on a per-customer basis the amount is trivial.

Imagine how much money an entity like UPS paid to develop and maintain similar mapping capability just 20 years ago – likely hundreds of millions of dollars. You probably purchased GPS displays for your vehicles a few years back, and now they are completely obsolete because you can just stick the "free" phone on the dash and it will tell you where to go.

These large-scale consumer-oriented innovations in technology have paved a path for you to assemble a portfolio of extremely cost-effective customer service applications. The biggest expense is the time you will invest to learn about the new breed of applications and build a strategy that suits your business goals and the customers you serve.

If you are the owner, a principal, or a top executive of a service contracting business, most of your time should be spent on customer relations, sales, staff recruiting, *and* innovations in customer engagement. The balance of activities in the company relating to daily operations should be delegated to staff so you have time to accomplish more than simply maintaining the status quo in your business. If you want to enhance the value of your business via innovations that differentiate your customer service, your time has to be allocated accordingly. Grinding away at internal operations will not set your company apart in the eyes of your customers. Remember the story of taxi management compared to Uber? Uber crushed the taxi companies because they focused on customer engagement innovations.

If you want to successfully use innovation to separate your business from the competition, you may need to alter your thinking about how you evaluate, acquire, and put Internet applications to work in your business. The new breed of Internet applications you will use for customer engagement are very different from the applications you purchased to manage financials and accounting. Customer engagement is very different from accounting, so it makes sense that you need different online tools.

As you evaluate and assemble your portfolio of customer engagement applications, consider these key ideas:

1. **Not one, but many** – You will have many applications from many vendors because no vendor has a monopoly on great customer service innovations. Look at your smartphone screen. Do you have one application or many? The only way to keep up with the pace of innovations demanded by your customers is to be prepared to adopt new applications instead of waiting on one vendor to update your lone application to address market requirements.

2. **Software as a service (SaaS)** – All customer-engagement applications are delivered in a SaaS or cloud model because no business is in a position to afford the infrastructure costs to do truly amazing things with technology on a standalone basis. The expense and rate of innovation are simply too great for a single company to bear that burden alone. When Amazon and others are spending billions on development and infrastructure why would you ever think about building something yourself instead?

3. **Loosely coupled integrations** – Because they are many and because they are SaaS, the applications integrate with other applications as necessary to enable seamless business processes and sharing of data. These integrations are accomplished by public application programming interfaces (APIs). Applications no longer share a database on a server. You do not need to understand how to read or use APIs, but you will ask the application vendor how their APIs work and what partners they support. More on this subject in chapter 9, "How to Identify and Purchase Quality Applications."

4. **Cheap and easy** – None of your applications should be expensive or difficult to adopt. If they seem that way, you are dealing with a poor vendor. Think how easy it was to set up your LinkedIn profile, an eBay account, Facebook, etc. Use these experiences as your guideline.

Consider the case of Team 360 Services in Indianapolis. Michael Crafton, the founder and CEO of Team 360 Services, tells a great story about the evolution of his company from one focused on technology for internal operations to being focused on best-in-class capability for each functional department – particularly customer service.

When Michael started the company in 2005, he began with a couple of simple PC applications for managing the business – Maximizer CRM and QuickBooks. Michael quickly realized the limitations of these applications: data was trapped in the office, and the applications did not work together effectively. So he embarked on a two-year project to implement NetSuite, a cloud-based all-in-one application for accounting, back office, sales, and customer service. With NetSuite his data was no longer trapped in the office, but aside from the accounting functions, no one else in the company was happy with the tools for their job. Turns out that NetSuite is a market leader in accounting capability, but all the other aspects of the platform are relatively weak when compared to best-in-class applications.

So Michael began pulling pieces of the solution out of NetSuite and replacing them with best-in-class capability for his particular type of operation. ServiceTrade was selected for scheduling, technician productivity, and online customer engagement. PipeDrive CRM was implemented to manage sales activities. TinderBox is now his sales presentation and electronic contracts platform. ADP is the application for payroll. Each of these applications is loosely coupled to the others where critical data must flow between them. Michael, however, also has the flexibility and freedom to "rip and replace" any particular application if it falls behind the market – without impacting all the employees at 360 with a massive upgrade to a new all-in-one system. Now his employees in each department can get the functional capability they need to be best in class in their work, and customers are happier because of the positive experiences they have with Team 360 Services.

The online retail revolution of the late '90s, along with related trends in personal consumer technology, foreshadow both the change and the opportunity for trade service industries. **Those companies that embrace the opportunity to build an incredible brand via Internet technology have the chance to do so at a price and pace unimaginable just 10 years ago.** Sir Isaac Newton once wrote in a letter to a contemporary physicist, Robert Hooke, that his latest breakthrough in physics theory had been enabled by the previous discoveries of others. "If I have seen further it is by standing on the shoulders of giants."

Today, as you face a market of customers who expect online engagement because they are accustomed to working with brands like Amazon, Google, Apple, and eBay in their personal lives, you have to decide if you are going to meet that expectation or be left behind. While these Internet, retail, and consumer technology giants have set the tone for customer expectations, their existence also offers you a ladder for climbing onto their shoulders to survey and engage your customers. You have the opportunity to "stand on the shoulders of giants" in order to accomplish for pennies what was unthinkable a few years ago even with a huge capital budget. **Your only real investment is the time and the will power to commit to innovation, climb the ladder, and take your service activities online to build profitable customer relationships that last forever.**

CHAPTER 7

The Digital Wrap: Using Service Activities to Create Online Impressions

Through the introduction and the first six chapters of this book, I have made the case that technology is going to redefine the landscape of service contracting. Parallel examples from other industries predict the future for service contracting. The trails blazed by these other industries also lower the cost and complexity for you to deliver similar innovations. Adopting new technology will be easier and cheaper for you. The balance of *The Digital Wrap* deals with practical advice, examples, and guidelines for building your digital wrap.

Let's start with reexamining why you wrap your trucks and vans with logos, brand promises, and contact information even when it can cost anywhere from $1,000 to more than $5,000 per vehicle. The answer is simple: as your techs deliver service you want both current and prospective customers to see your brand in your service area. Ideally the logo and the brand promise are memorable, and the simple act of delivering service yields future service opportunities.

Truck wrapping is a popular branding medium, and it is highly effective due to a couple of important principles:

1. It is ideally targeted because it only appears in the areas you serve. Except for joyrides by technicians on weekends, the impressions you deliver have a near 100% probability of being relevant to the audience.

2. It requires no extra effort by the technician. Delivering impressions through the wrap does not distract the technician from the most important task of delivering quality service to the customer. The technician does not have to remember to do anything extra to deliver these customer impressions.

The truck wrap works because it is targeted and easy to administer. Using these principles, how might you gain impressions in your coverage area as easily as with the truck wrap? What other simple artifacts of delivering good service, similar to simply driving the truck to the service location, might yield favorable customer and prospect awareness? How can you use technology to deliver exceptional customer service, uncover new opportunities with customers, and remain constantly visible in the online neighborhood so they know whom to call when service is needed?

The digital wrap delivers impressions to the customer (and prospects, too, in some cases) before, during, and after service appointments. A digital wrap, like a truck wrap, is simply a set of service activities that places your logo, brand promise, value proposition, and contact information in front of the customer throughout the service cycle. Just like the truck wrap, the digital wrap provides impressions without requiring anyone on your staff to do anything extra to gain the marketing value of the customer impression. Unlike the truck wrap, however, the digital wrap is more enduring and memorable because it is easily recalled; the customer simply searches their inbox or the Internet to find you again.

However, the digital wrap only works if you truly embrace a digital approach that does not incur extra steps on the part of your technician or your office staff to get the benefits. Remember one of the key principles of the truck wrap? No extra work is required to gain the impressions. Anything extra will be ignored in the chaos of everyday operations. Changing operations so that digital impressions happen automatically is the benefit of going digital instead of simply going paperless – updating the format from paper to electronic files (more on that later in this chapter). So what is the roadmap to going digital? What are the essential principles?

Here are the overarching guidelines of a digital wrap strategy:

1. Systematically collect and store customer email addresses and mobile phone numbers. Make this requirement part of every interaction with the customer. It should just be part of your customer service application. If not, get a new one.

2. Find opportunities to migrate processes like scheduling, dispatch notifications, job review, invoicing, and estimates/quoting online. NOTE: Electronic copies of your old paper forms scanned into digital format and attached to an email *does not make the grade.* That approach is just extra work in the office or the field and will simply be ignored by your staff.

3. Use photos, video, audio, and other rich media to spice up your impressions and engage your customer more dramatically in the service review process. Seek service management solutions that integrate these critical elements seamlessly, not as an afterthought to manual processes.

4. Collect and manage more information (equipment information, service preferences, key contacts, equipment-monitoring data) for each customer to provide better context for your communications and demonstrate your quality stewardship regarding their property and equipment. Let them be surprised by the thoroughness and organization of the engagement. Put all this information online for your benefit and for theirs.

The digital wrap is much more valuable than the truck wrap because it is sticky. When the truck leaves the neighborhood, the impression is only valuable if the customer can remember the logo, the promise, and the contact information. How often does that happen for your business? It is impossible to know because you cannot really measure the impressions. If you are lucky, the customer will snap a picture of the truck on their smartphone for later reference, making it digital and therefore sticky.

Similarly, telephone calls to arrange service-call logistics are not optimal because they are expensive for you and aggravating for the customer, and the engagement is not conveniently stored for recall at a better time – it is not sticky. At best the results of a call are a number in the call log of the phone (if you reached their mobile phone) and some notes on a desk or kitchen counter notepad. A digital wrap that reaches the customer at their email address and the service contractor at their web address is easier for everyone.

The digital wrap is a superior marketing tool because it is:

1. **Easy to search** – Customers do not have to remember much because of the power of email, mobile, and web searches. Your brand is always in the palm of their hand.

2. **Easy to store** – Customers probably will not throw away the electronic communication because it costs nothing to store it. They certainly will throw away the yellow copy of the handwritten triplicate form left behind by the technician.

3. **Rich and engaging** – On the web, the richness of the interaction can be extraordinary. Photos, audio, video, references, recommendations, and links to other items of interest all draw the customer into the brand and make you more memorable.

4. **Measurable** – Web engagement is easy to measure. The digital footprints of the customer through the online experience can be used to improve your response to their needs. You can see their level of engagement – their "clicks" – with your online records through modern tools like Google Analytics. ServiceTrade uses this trick to notify you when a customer has viewed your online quote.

5. **Affordable** – The computer processing power to deliver an impression via email is much less expensive than the labor associated with phone calls or the expense of actually showing up at a physical address. And computer memory, bandwidth, and processing power are getting cheaper every day and will continue to do so.

When you migrate your existing customer service administrative processes to a digital approach, you have the opportunity to deliver lasting impressions to the customer without any additional costs for advertising. **The "go paperless" call to action that so many technology providers squawk about completely ignores the benefits of truly digital customer service.**

This uninformed "go paperless" soundbite focuses on the administrative benefits of migrating from bad handwriting and expensive triplicate forms to electronic forms, ignoring the potential brand-building leverage of a fully digital approach to customer service. Electronic paperless forms are better from an administrative perspective – cheaper, faster, and easier to share and store. However, establishing these processes – phone calls and emails with document attachments that are generally not searchable – is only a modest improvement that does not impress your customer or make you much more valuable to them. It is also not measurable. You cannot "see" when your customer is reviewing your work because they are examining a file on their computer's hard drive instead of clicking a link online.

A key principle in going digital with service artifacts – scheduling notifications, technician arrival updates, after-service reports, online quotes – is to change where the customer is engaged. Instead of the limitations of a physical street address and even a phone number, a digital approach engages the customer online to lower the administrative burden of the interaction and increase the likelihood that the impression sticks with the customer.

Here are some examples:

- Email that a service has been scheduled with a simple button for the customer to "confirm" the schedule or, alternatively, to request changes if the schedule is inconvenient.
- Email that the technician is on the way, with a photo of the tech, estimated time of arrival, and services to be delivered.

- A post-service "Thanks for the business. Here is your online service report with helpful links to other resources you may find valuable."

- Digital quotes with photos and videos of impaired equipment and one-click acceptance of the quote pricing and terms with an "approve now" button.

- Online reviews generated from a link embedded in the after-service email summary.

- Service scheduling reminders with interactive scheduling wizards.

- Access to service history, outstanding or approved quotes, upcoming services, and related reports via your website.

- Email campaigns when customer equipment is nearing end of life suggesting that it will be less expensive to replace it before an emergency failure. Provide the service data to back up your failure prediction.

All of these relatively small online innovations add up to a customer experience that mirrors what the online retailers have done to attract and retain customers. In the online retail world, it is normal and expected that you have an account with stored and actionable information reflecting typical customer service actions. All the artifacts of the shopping and buying process are there – shopping cart, shipping notices, return instructions, reviews, complementary items, etc. Each time you purchase from Amazon you receive not less than three emails documenting and reinforcing expectations for purchase and delivery.

Expecting service contracting businesses to be held to a different and lower standard for customer service in the future is not reasonable. The digital wrap is your equivalent of the online account for retail customer service. It completes the shopping and buying experience for services and makes your company memorable and valuable beyond the value of the service labor.

The strongest benefit of the digital wrap approach to marketing is that your marketing and sales impressions are actually valuable to the customer instead of being an aggravation or interruption. Your company is perceived as being *attentive* instead of aggravating. You use data about the customer's situation to display your thoughtfulness and expertise with rifle-shot accuracy. An online quote with photos of impaired equipment, a link to a video referencing best practices in repair and the expected operational benefits, and the opportunity to approve with one click demonstrate your expertise. A phone call to follow up moments after the customer has finished reviewing the quote because your sales rep got a notification that the customer opened the link online is attentiveness instead of aggravation. An email that references past service history pointing to a pending failure and offering a value-priced upgrade during the slow season gets much more consideration than an annoying jingle on the radio.

Just as the truck wrap delivers impressions when driven through the service territory, your digital wrap delivers impressions by presenting your brand to the customer online. The digital wrap is just much stickier, and is targeted for response. The best applications deliver these impressions in a manner that does not burden your staff with extra work but in fact makes them more productive in helping the customer. More frequent and thoughtful impressions yield higher revenue from customer response and appreciation. **The most attractive digital wrap attracts and holds the most attractive customers.**

Now that I have reinforced the core principles of a digital wrap, the next several chapters outline key steps to take in adapting your business to be more competitive and choosing applications to enable your digital wrap. Most involve adopting certain technology capabilities, but some are about strategic decisions regarding expanding and updating your service offerings. All of the practical advice that follows is geared toward making your business more valuable by becoming more important to your customers through online engagement.

CHAPTER 8

The Basic Formula for an Effective Service Contracting Website

Throughout this book you've read about best practices and models for success from several other industries. These stories predict future trends for your service contracting business. The same basic formula holds true for website design as well. With a few tweaks specific to service contracting, successful models from retail and more advanced service businesses like banking can easily be applied to create a winning website formula for you.

Having a dedicated webmaster in your company is not practical, nor is it necessary. If you have a designated employee who understands how you want to present your image to the world and is capable of using LinkedIn or Facebook, you have all the necessary staff for managing your web presence. You are certainly going to work with a web agency for most of the heavy lifting in setup and search engine optimization (SEO). Therefore, you need to know how to hold an agency accountable to certain standards for your website. The goal of this chapter is to help you lay out a plan for communicating effectively about what you want your website to do for you. If you have a website currently, you will learn how to upgrade it to support your digital wrap strategy.

WordPress

Let's begin with the basic technology underpinning for your website. You should not consider any content management system for your website other than WordPress. It is by far the most popular content management system on the web. According to digital-statistics website expandedramblings.com, over 25% of all websites in the world run WordPress, and 50,000 new WordPress websites are added online every day.

This level of popularity creates network effects that benefit you. A *network effect* simply means that more people using WordPress make it more useful and valuable to you. Network effects are a primary driver of software application value because so many people are contributing knowledge and skills to the most popular applications. All professional web designers know how to use WordPress, so it is easy for you to find help. Also, thousands of developers are constantly updating the functionality of WordPress through direct contributions to the project and unique plugins that you can use. If you select WordPress, you can put all this innovation to work for your benefit.

If you are using a web agency, hosting company, or your cousin Vinny, and they are pushing you hard to use something other than WordPress, you should find a new website management partner. However, do not fire Vinny until your new web partner is on the job. The reason Vinny may be pushing something other than WordPress is so that he can lock you in to his services, and you may find your content held hostage if you fire him abruptly.

Basic Content

At its most basic level, your website tells the story of your business and your value proposition to your customers. If you do nothing else, be certain to at least tell the story in a manner that helps search engines deliver prospects and customers to your site. The basics include contact and location information, products and services, customers served, careers, and the team. Your site also needs to be mobile-friendly to rank effectively with search engines. Let's look at each of these basic elements in more detail.

Contact and Location Information

The contact information and the location of your business should be easily accessible and exactly identical in all the profiles you registered or claimed with each of the digital toll sites discussed by Bob Misita in chapter 5. Contact information such as phone number, email address, and a "Contact Us" link should be viewable on each page, maybe even in multiple places on the page. This information helps the search engines build the map back to your website from each of the toll sites where you registered a profile.

To see an example of how this works, check out the website created by Bob Misita's team at LeadsNearby for Tri State Fire Protection at getfireprotection.com. In the header of every page you see Tri State's phone number and email address. Along the right side of every page is a "Contact Us" form for submitting a request. The physical address and main office phone number are also displayed at the bottom of the site in the footer. This website easily meets the criteria of making it simple for the site visitor to get in touch with Tri State.

Products and Services

Each unique service or capability of your business should be represented on your site, ideally with supporting information and stories from customers and partners. If you represent manufacturers and equipment brands, be certain these are displayed and described with logos, photos, and stories reflecting a history of successful implementations and maintenance. If you have won any service awards or recognition from your manufacturing partners in the history of your company, tell those stories to affirm your "award-winning customer service."

In the past, the agency maintaining your website may have peppered your site with keywords in a manner that they believed was popular with search engines but perhaps was nonsensical to an actual visitor to the site. That was a common practice, but with the new search algorithms it is no longer effective. Review your site for clarity and simplicity. Avoid overly wordy and redundant content. Pictures and videos rank higher with search engines than plain text and, not coincidentally, with visitors to your site. Plus, they are a powerful way to tell the story of your business.

Visitor impressions made with images or video are much more memorable than dense textual stories. What was the name of the "terrorist plumber"? Likely you can remember that it was Mark-1 Plumbing because you can easily recall the photo of the truck with the anti-aircraft gun mounted in the bed. Go with images, video, and stories whenever possible.

Investing five to six thousand dollars on a professionally done customer-success video is probably a very good use of marketing expense. ServiceTrade has at least three of these on our site at any time, and they are our most popular lead source by a large margin. I also recommend that you consider producing a few of your own technology infomercials in which you give the customer tips and advice on simple things they can do to lower the repair and maintenance burden for their equipment.

When I am looking for advice about how to upgrade or repair my Ford F-250 Power Stroke, I always look for video lessons posted by enthusiasts and experts. Many of them are selling the parts and tools I need for the repair, and I often buy from them because their video helped me make an informed purchase decision.

You can post videos on both your website and YouTube to get the most bang for your effort. These videos draw traffic, and the amount of good will they generate with your customers will be reflected in your sales numbers. You become more memorable by digitizing your expertise. Sound familiar?

Customers You Serve

It is easy for prospective customers to know that you are the service vendor for them when a description of your ideal customer is an exact description of their company. If they can see logos and success stories from companies they recognize to be similar or identical to their company, it gives them confidence in their purchasing decision. The customer-success video described above under "Products and Services" can also be displayed in a "Customers" section on your website.

Do not be tempted to be vague or misleading about either your products and services or the type of customers you serve to attract a broader spectrum of web visitors. This information is harmful to your business in two ways: It drives the wrong visitors to your website, and it leads to disappointment when the wrong customer buys your services and you do a poor job. These customers will pan your business, either online or in their business circles. In both cases, misleading information and misguided web traffic lead to poor outcomes and brand damage.

Careers

Hiring technicians is tough. Since 2010, the annual Manpower Survey of Global Talent Shortage has indicated that skilled trades are the hardest positions to fill worldwide. Manpower defines skilled trades as "a broad range of job titles that require workers to possess specialized skills, traditionally learned over a period of time as an apprentice." You can find the Manpower Group's surveys online by searching "manpower global talent shortage survey."

Does the Manpower definition of skilled workers above sound like the folks you are trying to hire? If you want your hiring to be an easier process, putting up an attractive billboard on your website describing the folks you seek as employees will attract those folks to you. It is especially true that if you want to hire younger, technology-savvy technicians to fill future jobs, you need to present your company to them in a technology-savvy manner. The "Careers" section of your website, along with the balance of your digital wrap, is where those impressions should begin.

The Team

Customers like to know who you are when they contract with your company. Photos, short biographies, and training or certifications for each member of your team should be displayed on your website. You can crosslink these profile pages with the LinkedIn profile page for each employee to enhance the search engine optimization ranking for the profile pages. (I discuss LinkedIn in some detail in chapter 13.)

When you send notifications to customers regarding the scheduling of technicians or an update that the technician is en route to their location, linking the notification back to the page describing the skills of the technician and telling the technician's story makes your service more human and more memorable. Seeing a photo of the technician before he arrives at the service location creates a feeling of safety. It also reinforces the customer's confidence in the decision they made to contract with your company.

Mobile-Friendly

As of April 2015, Google began elevating the search-results ranking for web pages that are mobile-friendly above those that are not mobile-friendly. For two pages with the exact same content-quality score in Google's algorithm, the mobile-friendly page is listed ahead of the other page. It makes sense that Google would promote mobile viewability because more searches occur on mobile devices now than on tablets and desktop browsers combined. If the page has tiny text and needs to be zoomed and panned to read it on a mobile phone, that is not a good experience for the Google search user. So Google pushes those search results down the page.

If you want to check out how your site (or your competitor's) scores in mobile-friendly viewability, just search "google mobile-friendly test" and type in a page URL. Google will tell you how it sees the site and ranks it for mobile viewability. As with many other aspects of your website, you do not need to know how to make your website mobile-friendly, nor do you need to hire employees to manage it. You simply need to hold your web vendor accountable for mobile-friendly design. Use the free Google test to grade their efforts.

Advanced Content and Capabilities

Remember reading the best-practice stories from the retail industry in chapter 6? Those best practices are good guideposts for features that you should consider for your website as well.

Service Area Reviews and Check-Ins

Both online retailers and digital toll collectors use online review content provided by their customers to attract and retain new customers. In every service engagement with a customer, you should provide the opportunity for the customer to report unsatisfactory service to management or to leave a positive review on your website for great service. If you do not provide an outlet to bring management's attention to unsatisfactory service, customers will find an outlet for their frustration anyway. Whether it is some online forum or simply yakking to colleagues and acquaintances about your terrible service, your company suffers when you do not address bad customer experiences proactively.

For positive reviews, which should be the majority when all employees know the customer has the power to report on the service experience, give the customer an opportunity to share their satisfaction on your website. Each town, city, and neighborhood you regularly service should have its own dedicated "Reviews" page. This distinction is important because search engines like Google and Bing rank local search results ahead of other results that simply match key terms. For someone in the Royalton area of Cleveland who is searching for restaurant refrigeration repair, the area of your site that reflects reviews and service calls in the Royalton area is ranked ahead of other refrigeration service competitors in downtown Cleveland.

Similar to reviews, and co-located with review content, should be service check-ins. These are simply pinpoints on the map where you do lots of service along with service descriptions that help customers in those areas find your website. Google and Bing can see that you are popular in these areas, and your ranking will be very high for customers seeking a service provider in these neighborhoods.

Reviews and check-ins on your website are extremely important elements of your digital wrap. As with retail sites and the digital toll collectors, this content attracts visitors to your website and helps them make favorable purchase decisions for your services. ServiceTrade offers the ability for the technician to report check-ins and request reviews with essentially zero extra effort. If you do not enjoy these capabilities with your current customer service application, switch to one that provides these features and makes it easy for your technicians to use them.

Account History Content

Would you do business with a bank that does not provide you with the capability to see your account activity online? You probably would not even consider one that does not have a mobile app for managing your accounts, paying bills, moving money, and retrieving important documents. Why should your customers expect less from you? Your customers should be able to:

- See their service history
- Review the details of each job
- Pay you online
- Receive quotes and approve them
- Observe the full details of every service
- See service expenses for their key equipment

If your competitor offers all of these capabilities and you do not, how long do you expect to continue as the service provider of choice in your community?

When you create a digital wrap with your website, all the data and information trapped on paper documents in your filing cabinets instead become a sweet syrup that sticks customers to your business. It might seem like a daunting task to implement these ideas; don't feel like you have to do everything at once, but you should definitely have a plan to reflect your service activities and the associated data back to your website to hold your customers' attention.

Service Requests and Chat

If you are going to put up a billboard advertising your capability, shouldn't you also let your customers make service requests online? In the most advanced case, the request should allow them to use service history at their location to specify which equipment is malfunctioning so that you can respond in the most thoughtful manner – that is, with the right technician and the right parts. In the most basic case, simply populating a form on your site with information that is emailed to your dispatcher is certainly better than nothing. If your dispatcher responds quickly, which they should, it is highly likely that you will be the servicer selected to fix what is broken.

According to an Insidesales.com statistic, over 50% of online requests for new business go to the company that responds first. A study reported in *Harvard Business Review* found that companies that respond to an electronic request within an hour of that request are seven times more likely to be considered for the business than those that do not. Speed and responsiveness are critical.

Of course, the fastest response is immediate response via an online chat. Chat is a very simple application to add to your website via Olark, LiveChat, SnapEngage, PureChat, or any of a number of others that you can find and compare at g2crowd.com. You should not even have to think about which one is right for you because your web company should simply put it in place as part of their service. As with online service requests, make certain that someone at your company is engaged at all times during primary business hours (and even in some cases after hours) to catch customer and prospect requests. All of these chat platforms give you reports about how attentive your staff was to inbound chat activity as well as details about the engagement with the prospective customer.

Your website is a key component of your digital wrap. Moving beyond the concept of the website as a static billboard and instead embracing it as a dynamic extension of the services you provide increases the value of your business. Every day your business generates mountains of data – check-ins, customer feedback, failure codes, photos, measurements – that can be put to good use if you reflect them back onto your website for the benefit of your customers and prospects. All that information is worthless when it is trapped on paper forms inside your filing cabinets or in static files on a file server. Turn that information into gold that customers and prospects can mine online by going digital and inviting them to visit your website for a hassle-free, technology-enhanced service experience.

CHAPTER 9

How to Identify and Purchase Quality Applications

A foolish consistency is the hobgoblin of little minds,
adored by little statesmen and philosophers and divines.
— Ralph Waldo Emerson

In the very early days of ServiceTrade, I did some informal research into the software buying patterns of service contractors. My typical conversations with owners of small- to medium-sized service contracting businesses went something like this:

"So, Henry, tell me about any experience you have had buying software applications. I'm sure you use QuickBooks, or whatever you happen to be using for your accounting application. I'm interested in how you buy other software."

"Well, the only other application I have ever purchased is fleet tracking. I had it installed about eight months ago," Henry replied. I was happy to hear that he had been through a software purchasing experience recently.

I followed up with, "Cool. Fleet tracking is a good capability to have in your business. Your trucks are expensive assets, and keeping tabs on them, along with the driving habits of your techs, is a good idea. Tell me about how you decided you needed fleet tracking and the process you went through to evaluate vendors and pick a solution."

"The reason I wanted fleet tracking is because all the guys at the trade group seemed to be buying it, so I figured I should have it, too," Henry continued. "So I called up my buddy Jerry who runs a business pretty similar to mine. Jerry told me that he indeed had fleet tracking, and he liked it. So I reached out to his sales rep, Mike, and told him to send over somebody to install it on the trucks. Now, I don't really use it myself, but I understand it has been a real success for us."

"Henry, did you do any sort of evaluation of Mike's solution to be certain it was a fit for you?"

"Why would I do that? Didn't I just say that Jerry uses it? His business is real similar to mine," was his confused reply.

"Well, did you talk to Mike about pricing, or any other terms or conditions of usage, like the termination clause in the agreement? Did you do any comparison of other products in the market?" I asked, trying to pull some sort of detail about the process from Henry.

"Jerry bought it from Mike. That's all I needed to know."

This conversation would repeat itself again and again as I got deeper into the service contracting market. When buying technology for "tools of the trade" that was specific to their training, licensing, and the equipment they maintained, service contractors would undertake all manner of diligence, review, and exploration for value. However, software purchasing was a wasteland of shallow decision-making – and more often than not resulted in extreme disappointment. Service contractors have historically shown little interest in the potential of information technology as a critical element of their business. Paradoxically, however, I did find that their personal lives were often tattooed with all manner of technology and gizmos that rivaled the technology arsenal of any Silicon Valley wonk.

Bob Guthrie is a perfect example of this dichotomy. Bob is my fishing buddy who runs the quoting and repairs department for a large national fire protection services company. He is also the former proprietor of a sprinkler business that went belly up when Bob was too busy doing sprinkler work to pay attention to how the business was being managed by his partner.

On our way down to Oregon Inlet, North Carolina, on a fishing trip with my boat in tow behind the F-250 crewcab, I glanced back at Bob in the back seat. "What in the world are you doing?" I asked when I saw what was rigged up back there. It was approaching nine at night on a Thursday, and we were both taking the next day off. Bob had a laptop, an iPad, an Android phone, and a GPS unit arrayed around him in the back seat.

"Well," he explained "I have a couple of quotes that have to go out for approval to the customer tomorrow, so I am working those on the laptop. I am networked through the tethering feature on my phone. I am monitoring sea surface temperatures, ocean currents, and wind on the iPad to be certain we hit the right spot for the fish tomorrow. And I'm monitoring our ETA at that fleabag motel you booked us into again because last time we got there they had closed down and we had a helluva time figuring out how to get into the room. We will only get about four hours' sleep before heading to the boat ramp tomorrow morning, and I am not interested in sleeping in the back of the truck again."

Bob's former business down in Alabama had failed to a large extent because he could not be bothered with the details of the management systems, yet he is an absolute wizard when it comes to using technology to accomplish a broad range of things that interest him.

If you are the business owner or leader who loves exploring technology and looking for new tricks to improve your business, this chapter outlines a set of principles that should make both your explorations and your outcomes with new software applications more productive. If you are the owner or leader of a service contracting business and you HATE dealing with new business technology, read this chapter anyway. Then assign or hire someone to be the technology improvement leader in your organization, hand them *The Digital Wrap* as a guideline, and hold them accountable to its principles. Either way, the ability to evaluate and adopt a broad range of applications is critical on the path to building your digital wrap.

Here are the high-level core tenets of a successful software exploration and implementation in today's environment:

1. Understand why you want a new application. Outline a set of business improvements that should be achieved by this application.

2. Explore what is possible with a broad lens and an open mind. You might be surprised to discover many side benefits that you did not anticipate as you open your mind to a broad universe of applications.

3. Seek *software as a service* (SaaS). You may not have much in the way of SaaS in your business today, and that is okay. But the future of business applications lies almost exclusively in the realm of SaaS.

4. Be prepared to "buy many." You may have an instinct that an all-in-one solution is better and easier. Nothing could be further from the truth. Look at your phone screen. One app? Or many? You will use many software applications in your business going forward.

5. Buy from interesting people. Interesting people do interesting things. Be discerning in your evaluation of the vendor's management team.

6. Review pricing and other key terms. If you pay close attention, you can get more than you think from the negotiation. Be aware of tricky or deceptive terms and conditions. (We'll cover these to help you negotiate a better outcome.)

Each of these core tenets is reviewed in detail in this chapter along with a few simple frameworks for doing purchase analysis.

Core Tenet 1 – Understand Why You Want a New Application

The first step in making a thoughtful software purchase is to ask yourself two important questions:

- Why do I want a new/different application anyway?
- What improvements should we realize with new/better/ different software?

These seem like obvious questions to ask, and the answers should be simple, measurable, and lead to clear business objectives. You might not be able to correlate everything perfectly to the software capability, but you should nonetheless understand your goals around better business outcomes. The art in answering these questions is to achieve the correct level of *abstraction*. Here are some examples:

Too Abstract

- Higher profit
- Higher revenue
- Lower expense
- Higher morale
- Greater visibility
- Less paperwork

Too Focused

- Technicians can complete Form 72b 12% faster
- Accounts payable processing expense should be lower by 18%
- Submit paperwork for third-party management systems with half the effort
- Complete payroll processing online with half the office labor

Just Right

- Lower administrative costs associated with scheduling and invoicing
- Increase the percentage of quotes accepted by customers
- Increase weekly revenue per technician
- Lower travel time/fuel expense per $100 of service revenue
- Faster collections and lower accounts receivable *days sales outstanding* (DSO)
- Fewer overdue jobs and missed service windows
- Increase revenue from existing customers by 20%

If your goals are too abstract, you will not be able to efficiently link your outcomes to the new software capability – improvements (and failures) get lost in the noise of the business. If you are too narrowly focused, you might indeed accomplish your objectives with the software application while simultaneously degrading the business in other meaningful ways – you'll win the battle but lose the war. If you get it right, the business will be stronger overall because the measurements you picked are the really important ones. There will certainly be some negative consequences, too (that is, you will have a new monthly expense item entitled "software subscription expenses"), but these should be trivial relative to the big-picture improvements.

This list of objectives for new applications should have between three and six items. Any shorter and you will narrow your search and likely miss some opportunities. Any longer and you are stacking up features instead of defining business improvements. Features come second, after the business objectives are set.

Core Tenet 2 – Explore What Is Possible with Software

The list of objectives should be pretty firm before you begin your search for software; you need to understand why you are searching. The features you want, however, should be a joyful wish list that actually expands pretty rapidly during the early days of your search and then contracts as you work your way toward the reality of a purchase. I suggest you start building your initial list of possibilities with a fun session among *all* the stakeholders, completing statements like the following:

- "I really hate it when [describe some aggravating administrative snafu]."

- "Customers really get annoyed because _____ "

- "I waste so much time just trying to _____ "

This "bitch session" should lead to a long list of aggravating nuisances that you deal with every day. The inverse of these nuisances are the solution features you are seeking. Try to start with a list of about 10 to 15 items. Here are some good examples from ServiceTrade:

- Build daily schedules for the techs based on where the jobs are located on a map to reduce travel time between jobs.

- Let the techs record audio, photos, and video to describe how to fix an impaired piece of equipment instead of kidding ourselves that they will write it down. Eliminate the miscommunication and phone calls when the office is building a repair quote.

- Capture customer signatures electronically in the field to acknowledge the work that was delivered and agree to our warranty terms and conditions.

- Automatically notify techs of changes in their schedule without having to call them with every update.

- Send customers a link to all work delivered, including all electronic files and photos, so they can review the work without the office having to manually scan, attach, and email.

- See all tech activities on a dashboard so they do not have to constantly call the office with updates and jam up the phone lines so customers cannot get through.

- Bill jobs immediately after completion by the tech instead of waiting several hours or days for the paperwork to come back into the office.

- See all past-due jobs in a list so that we can confirm a schedule with the customer as soon as possible before the customer gets annoyed.

- File all activities associated with a customer location in a single electronic record so that we can do better customer service when the customer calls with an issue.

- Notify the customer when the tech is en route to their site and give an estimated arrival time using GPS data so that no one has to call.

As you begin exploring and reviewing what the market has to offer via demonstrations, trade shows, free trials, reference calls, etc., you will discover other cool things that can be added to your wish list. No one product has a monopoly on good ideas and good features. The corollary of this statement is that you will not get everything you can imagine in a single product. In fact, your exploration might lead you to buy multiple products across a span of application genres because you discover capabilities that you just cannot live without after seeing them in action. In any case, daydreaming about potential software features is a healthy exercise that your team should definitely embrace.

However, you should also do a couple of reality checks as you build your dream list. Use a spreadsheet to attribute a value impact that each *feature* should have on each major *objective*. I suggest something like a 1–3–9 set of values to create some dispersion among the impact sums. In this case, attribute the impact values based on the following scale:

- 1 – likely a benefit, but perhaps a secondary effect
- 3 – clearly beneficial and impactful
- 9 – definitely will solve problems and yield significant impact in this area

If there are features on your wish list that have no impact value on your objectives, you should ask yourself why you want them. Did you miss something in the definition of your objectives?

If there are features on your wish list that score off the chart in terms of impact value on your objectives, you should prioritize these features as "must haves" in the evaluation of your application alternatives.

Here is an example in spreadsheet format that shows how this exercise displays feature impact against business objectives:

BUSINESS OBJECTIVES	APPLICATION FEATURES	Enroute Notifications	Map Based Scheduling	Online Quoting	GPS Job Clock	Technician Scorecard	Online Service Reviews	Real Time Dispatch Board	Online Customer Portal	Online After Service Report	BUSINESS IMPACT PREDICTION
Reduce Scheduling Costs		0	9	0	3	0	0	3	0	0	15
Increase Quote Acceptance		0	0	9	0	0	0	0	3	3	15
Increase Weekly Tech Sales		1	3	3	3	3	1	1	1	1	17
Reduce Missed Appointments		3	3	0	3	3	3	9	0	0	24
Increase Existing Customer Sales		1	1	9	1	3	3	1	3	3	25
Improve Search Engine Ranking		0	0	0	0	0	9	0	0	0	9
Reduce Customer Attrition		3	3	3	1	3	3	1	9	3	29
FEATURE IMPACT SCORE		8	19	24	11	12	19	15	16	10	

Figure 2 – Business Objective and Feature Impact Scoring Matrix

As your wish list of features evolves, revisit the impact-spreadsheet experiment as a team and narrow your requirements accordingly. Remember, it is unlikely you will get every feature you want with a single application, so be open to multiple products or narrow your purchase to the highest-impact product based on high-impact features.

Core Tenet 3 – Seek Software as a Service (SaaS)

Unless you are buying design/CAD/CAM software or games, I cannot suggest more strongly that you DO NOT CONSIDER ANYTHING OTHER THAN *SOFTWARE AS A SERVICE*. As a service contractor, you do not want to:

- Manage IT infrastructure
- Support application infrastructure for your users

- Experience slow/no feature improvements because you cannot manage the maintenance cycle
- Connect mobile devices to your servers and troubleshoot the subsequent performance and bandwidth issues
- Plan or manage disaster recovery
- Cover the expense of server hardware
- Manage the network gateway and security authentication mechanisms
- Maintain the operating system and database
- Troubleshoot malware activities
- Hire or manage IT staff
- Be trapped by a product that is going nowhere

That is the easy part. Now for the tricky, more nuanced elements of your search for SaaS. Old server-based, on-premises applications do not simply wake up one day and *voilà*, SaaS is born. If your application was EVER an on-premises application, it will NEVER be a SaaS application; the vendor is hosting it for you. While there is some benefit to this approach, IT DOES NOT SCALE. They must still do maintenance and configuration on every server instance and every operating system instance for every customer they host. Clearly that is better than your doing it yourself, but you will still pay a high price in fees and lack of innovation for this reborn SaaS (that is not really SaaS).

You can ferret out the pretenders from the real SaaS applications by asking these questions:

- Ask the vendor, "Would it be possible for me to run this application on my own servers and on my network? Because I really do not trust this whole cloud and SaaS thing. I want my data here!"

  If the vendor says, "But of course. We only offer that SaaS stuff for folks who are less sophisticated than you. We will absolutely sell you on-premises licenses," you trapped them.

You used their sales instincts against them. Now you can show them the door.

- Ask the vendor, "Clarify something for me. Is my data going to be all mixed up and jumbled in with any other customer data? My data will be hosted on its own unique database server, right?"

If the vendor says, "But of course. We would never host multiple customers' data on the same database server," you trapped them. Show them the door.

But Is SaaS *Really* a Good Idea?

YES!! Just like commercial banking is a good idea. Do you store your money in a box under your mattress, or do you deposit it with a professional bank where it gets "all mixed up and jumbled in" with other customers' money? Do you ask the bank to provide you with a separate vault for your money? Of course you don't. That would be ridiculous. It is the same with SaaS. The professionals are in charge of your data. They manage the access to it, the security, the reliability, etc. They give you useful ways to manipulate and get value from your data assets in the same way a bank gives you online banking applications to do the very same thing with your financial assets.

Let me ask a couple of other questions to further make my point about data security and integrity: Have you ever shopped on Amazon and seen someone else's product choices in your shopping cart? Have you ever bid on an item at eBay and seen someone else's bid pop up instead of yours? Have you ever used AOL, Gmail, or Yahoo mail and found someone else's emails in your inbox?

Just like the bank and your financial assets, your content and data – what you own – is segregated by the computers from what others own. You get yours, and they get theirs. And just like stealing from the bank is much more difficult than robbing your mattress vault, stealing your data from a professional SaaS provider is much more difficult than stealing it from you.

A disgruntled employee can have your data and ruin your business if he is willing to kick down the door to your office and steal your server. Now imagine that same employee sitting in the truck outside the fifteen-foot-high razor-wire fence that surrounds Amazon's data centers. Which scenario makes you a loser?

Once you have dismissed the pretenders from the contenders with the trick questions above, you can get into the *really* nuanced issues associated with buying good SaaS software. Because access to the data is controlled through the user interface, you cannot just update data willy-nilly without actually using the application the way it was intended. This is both good and bad. It is good because you cannot really mess anything up and lose or corrupt data as you can with an application that allows you to access the database. But it is bad when you need to do things with the data that the application does not support.

A good example of an important update that might not be handled with a *graphical user interface* (GUI) is a routine, periodic data sync with another application. The way SaaS applications handle this requirement is via technology called *application programming interfaces*, or APIs. It is how one SaaS application accesses your data in another SaaS application. You should ask the vendors to show you their API documentation and to provide a list of common integrations that other customers have achieved. If the API is not public, that means it does not really exist. (Here is a link to ServiceTrade's API documentation: https://api.servicetrade. com/api/docs.)

You do not need to be able to read and understand this kind of technical gibberish from a vendor. Just examine the clarity of their explanations and look at the examples they give for integrations. Note the candor and simplicity in how they reveal their APIs and documentation to you. If all you hear is mumbling, confusion, or outrage, you are dealing with a poor vendor.

Core Tenet 4 – Be Prepared to "Buy Many"

One of the things that amused me most as I did my scan of the market for service contracting applications was the number of application companies claiming they could provide any service contractor an "all in one" solution. Most of these were application companies with fewer than 20 employees. Remember the story in chapter 6 about Michael Crafton at Team 360 Services and NetSuite? NetSuite has over 5,000 employees and spends over $100 million per year on research and development, and they cannot even be an all-in-one solution for Michael's company. How can a company with only 20 employees and less than $3 million in annual revenue provide you with everything you could need in the realm of technology?

Try another exercise. Look at your phone. I have an Apple iPhone 6S. Apple is the most profitable technology company on the planet. They spend over $8 billion per year on research and development, and their applications represent less than 10% of those on my iPhone. If they could do everything for me, why does my phone not have a single big Apple button that says "All in One"? It doesn't.

In a world where technology is racing forward every day, the idea that one company can monopolize all the good ideas and give you everything to be competitive is crazy. You will buy multiple applications to serve different purposes. The good ones will work seamlessly with the other good ones via APIs. Do not be sad that you cannot find one application that does everything, because if you did find it and buy it, you would certainly be sad two months later when you discover how it limits your business.

Core Tenet 5 – Buy from Interesting People

The best explanation I ever got for how to buy good software came from ServiceTrade's Director of Customer Services, James Jordan. I asked him how he was going to determine which customer support management software to select. He responded to me by saying:

> I am going to start with the company that has public customer references from other software companies that I admire. If those smart people went through a process and selected their platform, then I can probably be comfortable using the platform as well.

He only had to try one, and that was ZenDesk. He spent a grand total of four hours evaluating it before making the purchase decision, and we have been delighted with the outcome. He was "standing on the shoulders of giants" when he made his selection. Likewise, references from companies that you feel are leaders in your industry are an important element in making a decision. If other really smart people like you are using an application, you are likely making a good decision to use it also. Combine this kind of research with the techniques outlined above to be certain you are making a good decision.

Also look at the experience of the management team. Do the key people at the company have the experience and capability to serve you well? Are they likely going someplace interesting that you will enjoy? Do they say interesting and insightful things? Check out their website. Read their blogs. Check them out on LinkedIn. Ask to speak to the most senior person you can access, and have them tell you the story of the company. Is it interesting? Would you enjoy sharing a beer/coffee/wine/tea with this person and swapping professional stories? If the answer is "probably not," then they should "probably not" be your vendor. Seriously. Interesting people deliver interesting products. Boring people... well, you know.

Finally, if the vendor website is ugly and riddled with hard-to-read text and grammar errors, what does that say about the product? It will probably be ugly, hard to use, and full of errors.

Try out the application – not with the vendor hovering over you, but set aside some time to really review and use the product. Is it easy to navigate? Is the documentation useful? Was your support experience favorable? Not all products lend themselves to a free trial, but for those that do you should definitely invest your time to sample it. Be especially diligent regarding the mobile application functionality, because it is often the most difficult aspect of a product to deliver with high quality and high performance.

Core Tenet 6 – Review Pricing and Key Terms

Pricing

Ideally you can easily review the vendor's pricing on their website. If it is not readily available, ask the representative why they do not publish what they charge for the application. If you get a thoughtful answer, then it is probably okay to proceed. If you get a suspicious answer, either proceed with caution or show them the door.

Pricing should be easy to understand and it should align with your business interests. If the license charges increase as your business experiences a downturn, that is not good alignment. If you do not get pricing leverage and greater value as you scale up the number of users, that is not good alignment either. Your vendor should benefit from your success, but you should clearly benefit more. If the vendor does not operate according to these principles, you should find a different vendor.

Key Terms

The most important practical consideration regarding the legal terms of a license agreement is your ability to enjoy uninterrupted use of the software – the vendor cannot turn off your account provided you continue to pay the bills. Here are the items to review in their agreement:

1. Price Increases

Price can go up and it can go down. With software, it is difficult to say exactly what the market will do, but what your contract says should be clear. You will probably find a provision that indicates that upon renewal your price is subject to an increase of between 3–10%. As a practical matter, if you are enjoying the software, you may not have much leverage in the renewal negotiation to keep your price increase below the maximum amount, so negotiate it before you sign up for the first time. If you want a better deal later, you will probably have to give up something else – like a longer term for the renewal (maybe three or five years), upfront payments, reference calls, etc. Make certain you can live with the annual increase amount before you sign the first time.

2. Termination Policy

The basic premise of SaaS applications is that you can quit (subject to paying the fees you agreed to pay), but the vendor cannot quit on you. The vendor cannot capriciously "terminate for convenience" just because they do not like you for some reason, or because serving you has become inconvenient for them. Generally speaking, if you do not pay, or if you do something with malicious intent or in violation of the End User License Agreement, the vendor can terminate your subscription agreement/privileges. Otherwise you keep paying and the vendor continues to provide the application indefinitely.

3. Service Level Agreements

Most SaaS applications include a level of customer support that is defined in a Service Level Agreement (SLA). Think of it as the response you expect from a landlord when you are renting an apartment. If the air conditioning breaks, you expect someone to be working on it pretty quickly after you report it – *if* it is really hot and you are suffering. However, if what you report really does not have a big impact on you, they can be a bit more relaxed in their response without you feeling that you have been inconvenienced.

The SLA defines the nature of the vendor response based on the type of problem you report and the type of service you have contracted to receive. Most of these are written in plain English, so read through it and ask questions about anything with which you are uncomfortable. Unless you are a *really, really* big customer, it is unlikely anything will change, but you should nonetheless understand what you are buying. The best way to understand the vendor's customer service is to try it for yourself and quiz references about their experiences. Reading the contract is necessary, but it is not really sufficient to appreciate what you will get from support.

4. Warranty and Indemnification

All software vendors use essentially the same terms in these sections of your subscription agreement. The basic promise you get is that the application does what the documentation says it does. Given that most documentation is rapidly becoming videos of the application being exercised by a user, the logic is pretty circular. Again, the best way to know what you are getting is to try it and to ask others who use it. The vendor is responsible for making certain you can use it if you like it (they cannot take it away, and they have to fight anyone who tries to take it away), but they are not responsible if you do not like what it does. The application must be legitimate, but it does not have to be good.

Purchasing SaaS applications should be a very practical matter. If you know what you want and you know why you want it, your job in the purchasing process is to prove that it does what you want it to do. Your job is also to benefit from the experiences of others you admire – "stand on the shoulders of giants," if you will. After you have invested enough cycles to know what you want and to know what is possible, picking the right applications is a matter of a couple of experience proof-points, no "gotchas" in the terms or pricing, and being realistic about your expectations.

No product does everything, but you should be able to get everything you want if you are a bit flexible and if the applications are truly modern and well designed. Purchasing modern applications to build your digital wrap does not have to be painful, and it should not take years off your life. You might even enjoy it.

CHAPTER 10

A Checklist of Key Technologies to Start Using Now

Shawn Mims is the director of marketing at ServiceTrade. In a company full of geeks, he is the geek who is responsible for technology that helps ServiceTrade build connections to our customers. He is only six years into his professional career after earning an engineering degree at North Carolina State University, and he enthusiastically tries almost every trick and technology available to help ServiceTrade and our sales staff present interesting ideas to our prospective customers. I invited him to write this chapter on applications that you should be using in your business today because his knack for finding technology that is inexpensive and "just works" is uncanny.

Shawn presents a list of applications that will help you communicate with, collaborate with, and generally become more important to your customers. Notably absent from his list is any mention of accounting applications. You should have one or a couple, and they should be good at helping you control your business expenses and report revenue. These accounting applications will not, however, help distinguish your business in the eyes of your customer, and therefore any matters relating to accounting applications are omitted.

As the director of marketing at ServiceTrade, I spend a great deal of time engaging with customers to try to understand what is important to them. By knowing what is important, I can find ways to present ServiceTrade in a manner that speaks to their ambitions and needs. Unfortunately I often find that their vision of business technology is the very thing that stands in the way of achieving ambitious goals for their business.

Service contractors often express a desire for a single technology provider or application to provide them with every feature they might ever require. Further, their descriptions of what they believe should be accomplished by technology are grounded in the details of their current operations. These two biases often leave them stuck with unwieldy technology that limits what can be accomplished in the business to simply *speeding up* what they do already instead of *doing things completely differently to delight customers and grow the business*. So I have come up with a visual example from the web that describes the way many service contractors think about technology.

Go to your favorite online search engine and search for the following term: "*Wenger 16999 Swiss Army Knife.*" Click on "images" to see the photo of the most insanely complex pocket knife and multi-tool imaginable. It has 87 tools, performs 141 functions, and weighs in at 7 pounds. Do you imagine that it performs any of these 141 functions elegantly? Can you imagine a more unwieldy and useless pocket knife? Do you imagine that there might be functions and tools beyond those presented by the Wenger that you might find useful in your daily routine? For instance, it does not have a hammer. Also missing are any torx-style screwdriver bits. I could go on and on, but I have two simple takeaways for you from this crazy example. First, a single application becomes more and more unwieldy as you try to bolt things onto it that it was never intended to accomplish. Second, if you wait for your single application to do everything for you, you will miss out on all manner of tools that could potentially make your business better and your people more productive.

I used the Wenger example because I want to recommend multiple applications to you, and while most of these will never be "bolted together" into a single application, they will absolutely make your business better. None of these application "tools" will solve all of your problems. However, they will work together, like the tools in your toolbox, to effectively solve some of the largest challenges your company encounters.

I grouped them into three categories for review: Inbound Marketing, Outbound Marketing and Sales, and Operational

Efficiency. Each of these categories is important in making your company more effective at attracting and keeping customers by presenting a rich record of your capabilities and services at the lowest possible cost to you. Many of these applications are free. All prices are as of April 2016.

Inbound Marketing

In 2006, HubSpot coined the term *inbound marketing* to define digital marketing activities that attract prospects to you instead of engaging prospects through broadcast advertising and outbound sales activity. Inbound marketing is a critical piece of any successful marketing plan for service contractors and, when executed properly, leads to scalable business growth and margin expansion. Even if you are not aiming for aggressive growth, having a steady stream of inbound opportunity gives you the option to "trade up" to better customers by "trading out" your marginal customers. An inbound marketing capability with a strong web presence, a mobile-friendly website optimized for relevant search keywords, and online reviews alongside local business citations gives you options for dramatic improvements in your business.

WordPress – Website Content Management

WordPress is a popular website content management system that makes it easy to build and manage websites from templates so that you don't have to know programming code to get great results. WordPress was reviewed in some detail in chapter 8. If you are using a web agency to build and manage your website, insist that they use WordPress so that you can:

- Adjust website content if your agency cannot respond to your update requests quickly
- Easily switch agencies due to the widespread use of WordPress
- Take advantage of WordPress plugins such as LeadsNearby (more about LeadsNearby below)

Price: Free

WooRank – Website Analysis and SEO Tool

WooRank has a very handy, free website analysis tool that generates a report of the good, the bad, and the ugly for your website. WooRank primarily indicates aspects of your website that need improvement in order to enhance your search ranking on Google. For example, WooRank summarizes which keywords are effectively used on your website so you can make adjustments in order to better align with the keywords your prospects use when they search for a company like yours. Whether you manage the updates with a marketing director in your company or use an agency, you should be using WooRank to hold them accountable to continuous website improvements.

Price: Free (for basic page review)

Synup – Online Review and Listing Monitoring

Synup is a great tool designed to help improve your company's digital presence and visibility by:

- Summarizing and updating local citations on sites like YP.com and Manta. These citations play an important part in Google's search algorithms.

- Reporting on your rank in search-engine results from the keywords your prospects use to find your company

- Notifying and summarizing online reviews for major services such as Google and Yelp

Price: Free (with optional paid plan for advanced features)

LeadsNearby – Reputation Development for Local SEO

LeadsNearby's Reputation Builder service uses a WordPress application that helps the best service contractors showcase their great reputation on their own website and improve local search results. Through a simple email process, LeadsNearby compels around 40% of happy customers to leave a digital review for your company. Imagine the number of positive reviews your company would have if 40% of happy customers left a digital review.

To understand the impact this could have on your business, do a quick Google search with the following term: *"Atlanta electrician."* You may notice the same company, TE Certified Electricians, showing up again and again at the top of the organic search results due to their use of this platform. Considering that a paid link on those same pages costs up to $120 per click, TE Certified is benefiting substantially from their search-results placement.

Price: $29/technician per month (minimum of 5)

ServiceTrade – Driving Online Content with Service Activities
A key principle of the digital wrap is using service activities to drive marketing impressions. The fewer extra steps you have to take for marketing, the more likely it is that your marketing impressions will actually be delivered to your audience. In this case, ServiceTrade is integrated with LeadsNearby so that your GPS clock activities for measuring technician productivity also deliver LeadsNearby check-in activity to your website. With zero extra effort, your technician-monitoring application becomes your marketing content application because ServiceTrade works seamlessly with LeadsNearby.

Price: Free to $89/technician per month (depending on features)

Outbound Marketing and Sales

Both residential and commercial service contractors rely heavily on sales activity for growth. Where residential contractors rely on converting inbound leads, commercial contractors lean on a mix of inbound and outbound approaches. Either way, an organized approach across the entire lifecycle of sales, from prospecting to closing, yields not only more business but also happier long-term customers.

Google – Discover Great Prospects
Prospecting is the earliest stage of the sales process. Who are you trying to sell your services to? Google makes it extremely

easy to find the best prospects if you know how to take advantage of its powerful search features. For example, if you are a commercial HVAC and refrigeration company trying to find the best restaurants and restaurant groups to sell to, here are a few different search techniques you can employ:

- **Review and price** – The best prospective restaurants are likely to serve high-priced meals and get positive online reviews. Use the review and price filters to find these restaurants.

- **Site search** – The "site:" search feature can be used to search public directories such as www.manta.com. For example, you can search Manta for restaurant groups in Atlanta via Google with a search query that looks like this: *site:manta.com restaurant group Atlanta.*

- **Advanced search operators** – Further narrow down your search results by using other advanced Google search operators such as quotation marks for exact string matches and "–" to exclude certain terms. For example, you can search for the exact term "restaurant group" in Atlanta and exclude consulting companies with this search: *"restaurant group" Atlanta –consult.*

Check out google.com/advanced_search to give it a try.

Price: Free

LinkedIn – Find Contact Information

Now that you've targeted the companies you would like to pursue, it's time to find the correct contact and their information. Start by using LinkedIn's advanced search to search by title, company name, location, and any relevant keywords. Much like advanced Google searches, you can use quotation marks for exact string matches. Once you find the profile for the person you need to contact, use a Google Chrome extension such as Email Hunter (emailhunter.co) or FindThatLead (findthatlead.com) to unearth their email address.

Note: LinkedIn can also be used to find prospective companies through relevant searches. For example, searching for "restaurant group" in the keywords field, "CEO OR president OR owner" in the title field, and limiting to relevant locations returns very useful results. Check out this document for reference:

http://talent.linkedin.com/assets/Product-Pages/Training/TipSheet-BooleanSearching.pdf

Price: Free to very expensive (all features mentioned are free)

Pipedrive/Pipeline Deals – Manage Sales Activities and Prospects

Customer relationship management (CRM) platforms help organize and manage your sales pipeline. An entry-level application such as Pipedrive or Pipeline Deals is perfect for companies new to CRM, while platforms like SalesForce are a better fit for larger-enterprise sales organizations. These platforms house all sales-related contact information and tasks to ensure that no one drops the ball in the sales process. They also measure salesperson productivity. Email integrations make it easy to log communications to eliminate digging through emails to understand the last or next steps in a deal. When properly managed, these applications help any sales rep handle a higher volume of prospects, deals, and opportunities.

Pipedrive price: $12/user per month
Pipeline Deals price: $24/user to $48/user per month (depending on features)

MailChimp – Build Value with Customers through Email Marketing

MailChimp is an entry-level email marketing platform. Because of its widespread use, MailChimp integrates with many other applications including WordPress to collect contact information on your website and CRM application (like those previously mentioned) so that your company can easily broadcast marketing messages to prospects and customers.

Email marketing provides service contractors with an incredible opportunity to build tremendous value with both prospects and customers. Simple, targeted emails can endear you to customers and build trust. Here are a few effective email campaign strategies:

- **Predict the future** – If you predict the future of your customer's service needs accurately, they will be blown away. For example, an email campaign to customers warning them about possible equipment failures they can expect with changing weather lets them know you are looking out for them and acts as a reminder to call you when problems inevitably occur.

- **Provide helpful tips** – Tips that help your customer save money in the short run result in loyalty and an increase in average lifetime value across your customer base.

- **Offer seasonal discounts** – This strategy both fills the slow months with off-season work and builds strong relationships with your customers.

Price: Based on volume of email addresses; free for up to 2,000 contacts.

ServiceTrade – Maximize the Value of Your Existing Customer Service Data

Remember the Aardvark example at the beginning of the book? Service businesses often deliver the "product" to the roof, or the basement, or the equipment room, or inside the ductwork. Customers cannot necessarily *see* the value that was provided to them (although they can often feel, smell, or hear it). It is important for you to *show* them why they buy from you as part of your service and sales opportunities. In the case of a problem you discovered during a routine maintenance call, ServiceTrade makes it easy to record photos and audio that document the problem. Then it is easy to turn the problem into an online quote, with the photos, for the customer to review and approve. Because the quote is online, your salesperson gets an email from ServiceTrade when the customer is reviewing the quote, which makes it easier for your salesperson to make a timely call to answer any questions.

The data you gather about your customers in the ServiceTrade application can similarly be exported to applications like MailChimp to drive very specific and tailored sales offers to customers who own equipment that your service data says is likely to fail. By organizing the data according to certain manufacturer models, equipment age, warranty status, and service history, your sales activity becomes informative and insightful for the customer, increasing the chances you will get the sale. The information you use to serve your customer can also be used to initiate customer service requests on your website (through a WordPress plugin). ServiceTrade puts your service data to work in ways that make you more valuable to your customers.

Price: Free to $89/technician per month (depending on features)

Operational Efficiency

Although the primary focus of *The Digital Wrap* is online customer engagement, many of the same principles for application adoption can also be applied to operational efficiency. Do not assume that your accounting application and its related "add-on modules" are the only way to address internal efficiency goals. An all-in-one application is not necessarily the right answer for every efficiency problem. Here are a few examples of applications that can improve your internal communications and processes:

Slack – Chat Application for Teams

If you are still communicating with your coworkers via texts and one-sentence emails, consider the switch to Slack. Slack is a chat application that works on any desktop computer or mobile device. Slack makes it easy to chat directly with anyone on your team or communicate in predefined groups. We typically recommend that service contractors set up chat groups for every operational division. For example, schedulers and dispatchers should be in a chat group with the technicians in their division for quick communication across the entire team. This setup also makes it easy for technicians to communicate and lean on each other's expertise.

Price: Free

Google Apps or Office 365 – Office Productivity and Collaboration Tools

Strong opinions about these solutions can be found everywhere. Microsoft diehards swear by Office 365 and Google fanboys and fangals will forever be loyal to Google Apps. I can tell you that both products are great! What really matters is that they are both cloud-based products that enable your company to easily collaborate on documents and files so that you can focus on service delivery instead of server IT.

Price: $5/user to $12.50/user per month (depending on features)

Fiverr – Task Outsourcing

Fiverr is an on-demand, outsourced labor and professional services marketplace that can take on data entry and other administrative work that piles up in your office. Work is priced by the task, and can be done for as little as $5. At ServiceTrade, we use Fiverr whenever we don't want to tie up a relatively expensive customer support resource with data entry work.

Price: based on task

ServiceTrade – Administrative Scalability and Technician Productivity

Amazing customer engagement is only possible when the office and techs are organized, efficient, and productive. ServiceTrade offers scalability for administrative office functions related to service delivery such as scheduling, dispatch, and work-order management. Mobile capabilities for field employees provide the data they need to perform topnotch work and enable collection of rich information that demonstrates better customer service.

Price: Free to $89/technician per month (depending on features)

Unlike the Wenger 16999 Swiss Army Knife, the "toolbox" described in this chapter actually helps you effectively accomplish your company goals. Much like your toolbox at home, you will likely find a need for additional tools as new projects arise, and discard old tools that no longer meet your needs. As you hone your sense for quality as it relates to software tools, don't be afraid to try new applications that might help your business. Consider this chapter your starter set of tools for building the business you always imagined you could have.

CHAPTER 11

Expanding Services:
The Case for Artisanal Cheese

Why do grocers always place the bread, butter, eggs, milk, and other items for daily consumption at the back corners of the store? So the customer has to walk past craft beer, tasty snacks, soda, candy, fine wine, and artisanal cheese to get to the commodity items. Everyone knows how much bread and butter should cost because these items are everyday purchases, and grocers do not make much profit from these staples. Artisanal cheese does not face the same pricing pressure because it is a niche item. It is a treat that customers occasionally splurge to enjoy.

If you are a service contractor, offering the service equivalent of artisanal cheese is a great way to maintain growth and profit, as comparative price-shopping on the Internet inevitably shrinks the margins for "bread and butter."

Artisanal cheese, however, needs to be packaged and sold differently than bread and butter. Bread and butter are everyday purchases consumed independent of any sales pitch; the customer must buy them for sustenance. Artisanal cheese is not an everyday purchase. The customer might take it or leave it depending on their mood, so it must be packaged and sold as a high-value product for discerning palates. It is typically merchandised in a fancy wrapping in an attractive display that contains complementary items that likewise command a premium margin. It is offered in the context of the consumption habits of the customer, often with expert reviews that help the customer feel good about the purchase at the inevitable high price.

As the Internet shrinks the world and empowers customers with information about how much common service contracting items should cost, you will need to expand your service offerings beyond bread-and-butter services to include the service contracting equivalent of artisanal cheese. Any customary and routine service or equipment replacement that you present to a customer will be scrutinized via searches on the web.

Do this little exercise and search for a typical plumbing or HVAC service. When I search "water heater replacement cost" the top organic hits returned by Google are:

- Angie's List
- Home Wyse
- Lowe's
- Cost Helper
- Home Advisor
- Apartment Therapy
- Home Depot
- Yelp
- Sears Home Services
- Red Beacon

These are the organic search hits – the ones that Google claims are most valuable. The top ad-word paid hits are, of course, local plumbing companies. But if you are like me, you always ignore the paid ads and instead browse the organic search items to shop and compare for the real price information. Note that *all* of the organic hits on the first page for this particular search are aggregators of contracting demand or national distributors of water heaters. They are corralling customer demand to charge a toll on the bread-and-butter items you want to deliver. At a minimum, their prominent placement on Google with their pricing forces you to bracket your pricing. Until you can build a presence with customers and placement on Google using your digital wrap, these players set the rules on pricing for bread and butter with their online capability.

Of course you still want to deliver these lower-margin, bread-and-butter services to keep your competitors out of your best customer accounts. If you are regularly contacting your customer online with maintenance program information, an email campaign with seasonal tips, online service reports, etc., you will be top-of-mind for the repair or replacement call. Your company will be easy to reach by searching their inbox, and you will have first crack at the bread-and-butter service call before the Internet brackets your value. Bread-and-butter items can also be your entre into new accounts. Your best profit margin, however, comes from offering an array of services beyond the bread and butter. The broader your range, the more opportunities you have to sell into your customer base and achieve higher profit margins.

What are the artisanal-cheese items in your sales bag these days? Are you carrying any fine wine, craft beer, or tasty snacks to complement the bread and butter you are selling? Here are some ideas to consider for developing higher-profit artisanal-cheese service offerings:

Preventative Maintenance Programs

A preventative (or proactive, as some folks prefer to call it) maintenance program creates an explicit connection to the customer for which you get paid. It is a marketing program that you are PAID to deliver. You agree to perform certain services at routine intervals to maintain optimal equipment performance. The customer pays for these services, and you get the opportunity to engage them online multiple times to schedule the service, confirm the service call, review the service performed, and perhaps consider upgrades and improvements based on your technician's observations. All this online engagement is in addition to the work that you actually perform on their equipment and the impression that your service technician makes onsite.

Do not measure the value of preventative maintenance solely on the margin from each individual visit. Yes, you need to put in place productivity capabilities such as a map-based scheduling routine and online schedule confirmation to avoid extra expenses associated with delivering and administering maintenance programs. These programs are definitely profitable if you use technology and thoughtful processes to manage them. The real value, however, is the systematic customer engagement driven by the contract. You are creating a bond that puts you first in line for all service opportunities related to your expertise. It is up to you to provide broad expertise, thoughtful observations, and online engagement to harvest the best profit from these marketing activities.

Do not assume that your technician has to go onsite for every preventative maintenance service call. You can sell a filter-replacement service that is self-service for the customer. The customer is performing the work, and you are the expert who oversees the work – online of course. In ServiceTrade, you can easily set up the service interval with the parts needed and assign the customer as the subcontracting company delivering the work. When the filter replacement is due, your customer gets an email with a link to the job in ServiceTrade. Attached to the job is a video of their location demonstrating exactly how to replace each filter. The filters arrive to be installed based on shipping arrangements you have made with the parts supplier. You then get alerts and notices back in your office regarding the completion status of the replacement, including photos of the new filters installed correctly and any comments the customer employee may have made, whether written or audio or even video. You were paid to be the expert and add value, but you incurred zero technician labor costs associated with delivering a great outcome for the customer.

Here is another great example of proactive maintenance from outside the service contracting market. Discount Tire offers free rotation and balancing for all cars in my household, regardless of whether I bought the tires at Discount Tire. I have purchased several sets of tires from them. But when I bought my daughter a car, the tires on that car had not been purchased from Discount

Tire. Nonetheless they are happy to have her stop by the location to have the tires examined, balanced, and rotated. This engagement gives them the opportunity to sell the next set of tires to me when they discover my daughter's tires are nearing the end of their useful life. The balance service is fifteen minutes of fill-in work that falls into the category of marketing expense for them.

Equipment Monitoring

Along with a preventative or proactive maintenance program, consider ways that you can add value (and reduce costs) to that program by monitoring the equipment for the customer. (More details about this in chapter 12.) Consider the bread-and-butter water heater replacement. Think about how you might instrument the water heater to detect a leak condition or a cold temperature condition that would be a painful and aggravating disruption for the customer. Offer to set up the equipment in a manner that gives you both visibility and potentially some remote-response capability to address the issue before it becomes a huge hassle. With equipment monitoring, the customer is paying you to be the expert so they can avoid hassles that they are ill-equipped to manage, and you have established yet another connection to the customer through which you can demonstrate value and keep your competitor and its marketing campaigns at bay. When you have a high-tech connection to the customer that informs you of everything happening with the equipment, the competition never gets a shot at the business.

Extended Warranties

Have you noticed that auto dealers and places like Best Buy offer an extended warranty with the purchase of almost every piece of equipment they sell? Have you noticed that manufacturers are offering longer warranties at the time of equipment purchase? You should be the expert engaged with the customer at the time of equipment purchase, and you should consider offering an extended warranty and pocket that money yourself.

However, to do this well, you need to do some research. It doesn't make sense to offer a warranty service without understanding the potential costs and profits, so you absolutely must have data that defines the failure potential for the equipment. Find out:

- What is the likely mean time to failure?
- Which parts are likely to fail?
- What are the exclusion conditions?
- What is the remedy for the failure?

Study the manufacturer's terms and pricing. Review data from all your other customers who use that equipment. Stock the parts that can potentially fail, and routinely replace them during your preventative maintenance if a quick and easy part replacement might prevent a catastrophic failure. Have the customer explicitly agree to your terms and conditions via an electronic, online contract process – one that guarantees you will not lose the contract in some filing cabinet in your office.

The ideas above might not be perfect fits for every service contracting business, but surely there are artisanal-cheese opportunities in your business that can provide margin as the price of bread-and-butter services shrinks due to comparative price-shopping on the Internet.

Remember that the demand for artisanal-cheese items is different from that for bread-and-butter ones, and they must be packaged accordingly for you to close the sale. Do not expect a technician to just show up and scribble a couple of cryptic codes on a triplicate form and grunt "this is how I fix it" to the customer and that the customer will sign up for your artisanal-cheese program. Present the valuable items to the customer in a "fancy package" with all the "quality ingredients" and "expert reviews" highlighted. Ideally it should be a digital presentation on your website that documents the benefits and approach with statements from customers who bought it and loved the outcome. Consider a product like TinderBox (gettinderbox.com) for making this presentation and recording the customer's signature agreeing to your terms.

When you expand your offerings to more broadly engage the customer's service "palate" with artisanal-cheese services that are more appealing than simple bread-and-butter ones, your business will grow. Even better, your profit margins will increase even in the face of aggressive Internet marketing by your competitors.

CHAPTER 12

Smart Services, Monitoring, and the Internet of Things

The "Internet of Things," or IoT, is just a fancy term to describe connections to the Internet that are not humans staring at screens. Whether it is an expensive Tesla car sending performance data for managing maintenance services, or super-cheap temperature and current sensors measuring the performance of an ice cream cooler in a convenience store, more and more new connections to the Internet are "things" instead of people. These connected things can provide direct connections to customer equipment to help you deliver smarter services. The folks in the fire and security alarm industry have long benefited from the high margins that monitoring contracts deliver to a service contracting business. Now the expanding array of connected equipment can lead to monitoring contracts and support services for many different types of service trades.

To demonstrate an example of the IoT revolution and how it opens new opportunities for service contractors, I invited Jay Fiske from Powerhouse Dynamics to write this chapter about smart services. Jay is a friend and an alumnus of the same fellowship program I completed at MIT. His company, Powerhouse Dynamics, has developed a system called SiteSage that consists of a SaaS application with Internet-connected controls and sensors for small-footprint buildings (less than 20,000 square feet). As a service contractor, you can use applications like SiteSage, coupled with your expertise, to provide valuable monitoring and support services to your customers. I call these IoT-enabled services "smart services."

Earlier in *The Digital Wrap* Billy highlighted technology trends pioneered by the online retail and consumer technology companies. Those technologies paved a path to the low-cost capabilities you have access to today: SaaS applications and mobile platforms you can use to serve your customers better. There are trends being driven by consumer demand and other large-scale technology initiatives that similarly open the door for offering smart services to your customers as part of your broadening service portfolio. You can now offer customers with smaller facilities reasonably priced, technology-enabled services that were historically only available to large-scale, capital-intensive building operations.

There are three technology trends that make monitoring and smart services affordable realities for you and your customer base:

1. **Low-cost wireless controls and sensors** – The explosion of connected consumer devices has dramatically reduced the cost of wireless controls and sensors. For example, almost every mobile phone and all smartwatches and Fitbits have a wireless accelerometer. Wireless temperature sensors are everywhere. High-volume production leads to low prices for these devices, making them economically compelling for commercial applications. Installed at your customers' facilities, these devices reliably connect to the Internet to provide insightful data and remote control over HVAC, lighting, and other systems.

2. **The Internet is everywhere** – Nearly every building today – even the smallest commercial facility – has an Internet connection. If it doesn't have one today, it will probably have one soon. In many cases customers of businesses are driving the need for connectivity because Internet hot spots attract and hold customers. Being able to tap in to these existing connections lowers the cost of connectivity to nearly zero.

3. **Cloud-based software/SaaS** – As discussed extensively in this book, because it does not require software that is constrained to a single local PC, cloud-based software provides you, your technicians, and your customers with persistent access to data and controls from anywhere. With SaaS applications, no one in your organization or the customer organization has to

manage the complexities of a data center to enjoy the benefits of a smart-services application. SaaS gives you hugely capable systems at very low cost.

Powerhouse Dynamics provides one such SaaS application: SiteSage. Service contractors who want to extend their maintenance and repair services can use SiteSage to provide equipment-monitoring and energy-management capabilities. SiteSage helps companies that manage large numbers of smaller commercial facilities, and service contractors can use the application as part of their digital wrap strategy. The application helps you provide a broader value proposition based on data, expertise, and Internet connectivity, and you become more important to the customer. Remember the "artisanal cheese" lesson regarding proactive service agreements and warranty plans? An application like SiteSage can help you fulfill your promises around these offerings through remote monitoring and performance reports. Your warranty service can be much more profitable if you detect and remediate performance issues before they become catastrophic failures.

When you combine an easily deployed SaaS solution with low-cost wireless controls and sensors that constantly feed data to the application over inexpensive Internet connections, you can deliver a whole new range of capabilities never before available to small commercial facilities. These new capabilities extend far beyond simply managing the energy consumption of a building – they give you opportunities to delight your customers.

You can spot trends related to both equipment performance and employee behavior that make you a valuable partner to your customer in their efforts to save money, prevent disruptions, and even lower their carbon footprint as a responsible corporate citizen.

Opportunity: Your Focus vs. Your Customer's Focus

In the early days of Powerhouse Dynamics, we focused on the residential market. We learned that 80% of the people who put programmable thermostats in their homes do not program them.

If you've ever tried to program the thermostat in your home, you already understand why. Most programmable thermostats are poorly designed, have programming menus that require the user to have an advanced engineering degree, and are not accessible anywhere other than at the thermostat itself. Even if the thermostat was programmed, it only takes one uncomfortable family member to override the program permanently, eliminating any energy savings.

While the residential market was interesting and fun, we discovered that there is a far more urgent need for SiteSage in the commercial realm, specifically among companies that manage a large number of smaller commercial facilities. They were losing substantial profits due to an inability to effectively manage and maintain their HVAC and other critical equipment, which made the economics of investing in our system very compelling. So we shifted our focus to the commercial world.

When we made this change, we discovered that the same people who weren't programming their thermostats at home also weren't programming them at work. And the problem at work is much bigger because even a small commercial facility uses far more energy than a typical US household. When the thermostats aren't programmed, or when a staff member can permanently override the set points, they're likely blasting air conditioning in the summer (or heat in the winter) all night long when there are no employees in the building. Not only does this throw profits out the window, the excessive run-time of HVAC equipment accelerates wear-and-tear and shortens the life of this important and expensive asset.

The lesson from these experiences – both residential and commercial – is that most customers will not manage an application that optimizes energy consumption or lifecycle costs. It is simply not their focus. Humidity, set points, amps, pressure, short-cycling – you name the jargon – are not their bailiwick. These are the terms of your trade, and you love this type of data because it gives you actionable insights that you can relay to the customer. You are the expert with the data, and you can give the customer the performance outcomes they desire for their valuable property and equipment. This is your focus.

With applications like SiteSage, you can solve problems for your customers *without having to roll a truck to their site.* Your technicians and customer service team can control tens, hundreds, or even thousands of locations' heating and cooling systems (and other systems, too) directly from tablets, laptops, and smartphones. You can use the data and your expert observations to provide thoughtful recommendations for reducing operating costs. You can offer an expert monitoring and support service that interprets data and relays recommendations to the customer to help them optimize performance and save money.

If you can offer your customer a service that pays you more because they are paying the power company less, that is a tradeoff that can be profitable for both you and your customer.

Data Makes Invisible Problems Visible

Your customer is not focused on their equipment and its upkeep the way you are focused on it – that's why they hire you. It is generally not their job to be thoughtful about managing the infrastructure; they are focused on serving food or stocking shelves or serving customers. Because of this and because they lack data on equipment performance, most customers have equipment that is underperforming in ways that are adding unnecessary risk and cost to their operations.

A recent University of California at Davis survey of commercial HVAC equipment revealed that more often than not, HVAC equipment is not operating as efficiently as it could be due to problems from a variety of components, including:

- Refrigerant circuit
- Economizer
- Air flow
- Thermostat
- Sensors

In fact, some problems are so common they're more likely to be present than not. If you're an HVAC tech, you probably already know this is true.

For example, in two out of three HVAC units surveyed by UC Davis, the economizers were broken. When the economizer isn't working, it won't be obvious to people in the facility because the rooftop unit can still deliver air of the proper temperature. However, it does so by consuming far more energy than necessary. This is just one small example of how invisible problems can lead to unexpected expenses.

When we install our monitoring system with a new customer, we frequently discover hidden problems. As an example, our software and sensors detected that a new rooftop unit at a customer site (a national retail chain) was behaving in a strange way: it never shut off. We alerted our customer that they had an issue. Because their system was still under warranty, they contacted the HVAC manufacturer, whom we will not name here! The HVAC manufacturer sent technicians out twice, and each time they claimed the system was working perfectly. The data from SiteSage said otherwise.

On the third try, the customer brought in a different technician not affiliated with the HVAC equipment manufacturer. The tech found a switch inside the unit that was stuck in the "on" position, confirming what was obvious from the data and automated alerts we were receiving; it was running 24/7/365. And this wasn't an inexpensive issue. The continuous operation of this rooftop unit would have cost the customer over $4,000 per year in excess energy consumption if it hadn't been detected and corrected. When you can discover this type of issue, fix it, and then demonstrate to the customer in your reporting that you just saved them $4,000, you have become far more valuable to that customer.

The bottom line is the HVAC world is *full* of invisible problems. These are not exceptions; these are the norm. Find them and fix them for your customer and you help ensure that their facilities are comfortable, they save money on energy, and their equipment lasts longer. You become the hero to your customer because you are the connected expert who is watching out for their important equipment and property. You have made invisible problems visible, and the results you deliver to your customer are valuable to them. The data delivered by monitoring applications combined with your response to your customer is one more element of your digital wrap.

Practical Steps to Get to a Monitoring Solution

All of this sounds great, right? But what are you going to do to move more of your value online through a monitoring solution for customers? The first step is to think differently about your business. Your job is to get paid for what you know instead of getting paid for where you go. Sending technicians to customer sites to turn wrenches is only a part of your business. Helping customers get the maximum performance and utility from their equipment and property is your primary responsibility, and any service you can sell that helps you accomplish that responsibility is the definition of your business. Below are the steps to follow to put IoT to work for you and your customers.

Explore, Connect, and Learn

Billy quoted Peter Drucker at the beginning of chapter 2 to make the point that a business exists to create and serve customers. Here is another great Peter Drucker quote regarding marketing and innovation:

The business enterprise has two – and only two – basic functions: marketing and innovation. Marketing and innovation produce results; all the rest are costs.

IoT is an area for marketing and innovation in service contracting. Invest some of your time in learning and trying things to come up with a new service product. Set aside some time every week or month to network and explore in this area. Seek out new products and applications that you investigate and reference with customers of the product. Some may be entirely outside of your particular trade domain, but you might be able to "twist" them to be totally appropriate for your customers and your value proposition. Look for "get started" kits that you can play around with to formulate a potential value proposition for your customers.

Beta Testing

In the software and technology world, a beta test is a prelude to a new product introduction. It helps you discover what the customer values, how you will support the product, and how to sell it. When you find a new technology that you think can add value to your business, pick one or two of your good customers and ask them to allow you to run a beta test on a few of their locations. Do not focus on profitability with your beta testing. In fact, you should probably absorb all of the costs in return for your customers' investment of time and energy to help you understand whether or not they find the technology helpful. Until you know what you are doing, charging them a fee would be a liability to the learning process. It may take several months or longer for your beta testing to identify the specific capabilities that truly delight the customer. When you understand what the customer values and how to deliver it, you can build a product plan for rolling it out to many customers as part of your services.

Think like a Software Company

There are three key elements to a modern software-company business model: consulting/training, subscription licenses, and support. Your new service will look very much like a software product (in fact you will be selling a software product). Your setup and configuration of the technology, along with any training you provide for the customer to teach them how they can use the application, is the consulting and training. You might make some margin on this activity, or you can give it away to lock in the subscription and support contract.

The subscription and support elements are often tied together and represent a set of capabilities and activities that help the customer maximize the value of the application. You make a commitment to the customer to assure the reliable performance of the application, monitor the data for fault conditions that create performance or expense risks, remediate the fault conditions (or advise the customer how to do so), and review the data regularly to provide a summary of recommendations at monthly, quarterly, or annual intervals. You are also available for questions and support requests the customer submits as they use the application.

Pull It All Together

Following is a practical example of how you might implement a successful monitoring service rollout after you define the value proposition with some customer beta testing: First, pick a person from your organization to be the product leader. Find someone who loves technology and is great at customer service. Ideally it is someone who can cover all aspects of the product lifecycle – the installation, training, alert response services, and regular reporting and proactive recommendations. Let them "own" the product. Work directly with the product leader to sell the first few implementations; do not expect your sales team to take on a new product until YOU know how to sell it and can teach them.

Set up an annual contract with the customer for a monthly fee (or they can pay up front), and establish the specific reports and engagement they will receive: application interfaces, alert responses, weekly performance reporting, and quarterly/annual recommendation summaries. Also set an internal goal for new sales and revenue for the first year. Do not expect optimal margins during the first year. If you cover your costs *and* the customer renews the service and expresses happiness after the first year, you can scale out aggressively to drive margin in subsequent years. There is nothing like a strong customer reference to drive more deals.

A successful monitoring and support product should drive a 50–70% margin for your business at scale. A monitoring and support specialist who costs you a fully loaded $100K per year should be able to manage $200–$400K in annual, incremental business from the monitoring and support services. This revenue will take the form of subscription monitoring and support fees, alert responses that lead to repairs and upgrades, and proactive planning reports that lead to upgrades and new installations. Your monitoring might in fact be a *loss leader* that simply places you in front of all repair and upgrade work in a proactive manner that delights the customer. It might be an expense that you associate with a very-high-margin warranty service.

The total revenue and margin across this portfolio of artisanal-cheese smart services, however, should be in the ballpark outlined above because the customer views you as the only choice to do the job right. You have refocused their attention from an hourly rate to business outcomes and savings. You bring incredible insights that lower expenses in other areas of their business, and their impressions of your business are no longer limited to the period when your truck is in the parking lot.

CHAPTER 13

LinkedIn:
Another Free Connection to
Your Customers

Imagine a new, digital billboard on the side of a super-highway. It's a high-tech billboard with videos and graphics all about your service business. You can direct traffic towards the billboard by extending invitations to travelers and by joining caravans of like minded explorers.

LinkedIn is one of the most important social media sites for professionals and businesses. It has great potential to connect you with current customers and potential customers as well as colleagues and other business leaders who are your potential partners.

You may be rolling your eyes at the idea of spending time on social media. Read this chapter with an open mind and consider assigning one of your office or marketing employees as your company LinkedIn expert. This is a great task to delegate to a younger member of your staff who is comfortable with and excited by social media. Your marketing or web agency should also spend some time curating and cultivating your LinkedIn profile as outlined below. You do not have to become a social media maven to get lots of value from LinkedIn.

LinkedIn is like Facebook for professionals and businesses. If your business is heavily weighted toward residential work, Facebook is probably a good place to have a presence for your business. However, no matter what your specialty or focus, every service contractor should have a LinkedIn profile page for their business and for each employee. Not having LinkedIn profiles for your company and employees is like not being in the phone book or the Yellow Pages 25 years ago. It is unthinkable. It should be a policy in your business because the businesses and people on LinkedIn are generally regarded as the best and most professional in their industries. It is one more opportunity to demonstrate your professional expertise and establish yet another digital connection to your customer. It is free at the basic level, so there is no reason not to take advantage of the platform.

The goal of LinkedIn is fostering professional connections. You can make connections to other business owners, professionals in your industry, and leaders in your community. LinkedIn is a global platform, but it can also be used to make connections in your neighborhood. Want to connect with the president of the Chamber of Commerce in your city? Look on LinkedIn. Looking to expand your book of business in a nearby city? LinkedIn has a search function that can help. Interested in networking with a speaker from your latest industry conference? LinkedIn would be the best way for you to forge that connection.

The Two-Way Billboard

Like most things on the Internet, LinkedIn is an interactive application. Using the billboard metaphor from above, when folks on the Internet highway wave at your billboard, you can recognize them and wave back. You get a photo of their "license plate" and some basic "vehicle registration information" in order to identify the "driver." Similarly, you can wave from the billboard, and it is easy to see when drivers wave back at you. It is the same basic trick that ServiceTrade uses to notify you when your customer has viewed your online quote. Remember that a digital wrap is better than a truck wrap because it is measureable. By tracking online "clicks" and "views" in LinkedIn, you have the opportunity to be timely and thoughtful in your response to customer interest.

Let me give you a concrete example related to the publishing of this book. Every week I get an email summary from LinkedIn informing me about activities on my LinkedIn account. One of the items LinkedIn reports to me is who has viewed my profile. I can also check this information anytime I like from the LinkedIn site. Generally I will wave back by reviewing the profile of those who have driven by my online profile billboard. In one case, someone from Ecuador in the book publishing business had reviewed my profile. Isn't it interesting that I was actually in the process of deciding how I was going to get *The Digital Wrap* written and published?

When I reviewed the profile of Lynne Klippel, the owner of Thomas Noble Books, I was intrigued. So I did some more research by visiting her website and reviewing information about other books and customers her company has helped – her online customer reviews. I went back to LinkedIn and reached out to Lynne for a conversation, which she accepted.

When we spoke, I asked Lynne how she came to view my profile. She told me that she regularly does advanced-level searches on LinkedIn for certain key words to find potential customers. Sometimes she reaches out directly, and other times she simply reviews the profile and stores the information for later marketing activities.

In a similar way, you can spend cycles on LinkedIn searching for customer profiles in your service area. You can also do direct advertising campaigns on LinkedIn according to the same criteria that you would ordinarily search and review. When prospects see your digital wrap in their LinkedIn neighborhood, and if they are seeking services like those you offer, it is easy for them to review you by following your LinkedIn profile back to your website and your company.

None of this works, however, if you and your company are not on LinkedIn. The balance of this chapter is dedicated to a few simple guidelines and tips for getting started on LinkedIn.

Best Practices on LinkedIn

To get started on LinkedIn, designate an employee to set up a free company profile. Include photos, video, and a full description of your business. Use common search terms and include a link to your website, physical location, phone number, and email address. Make it easy for people to connect with your business.

Similar to the toll collectors, LinkedIn operates on an advertising model that charges you tolls for traffic. You can pay LinkedIn for advertising or to get more information about folks you find interesting, but that is not our focus here. Our focus is creating one more reference point, or roadmap, for the Internet search engines to use in promoting your company.

Create Your Company Profile

Before you set about creating personal profiles for each of your employees (covered later in this chapter), you should first have a company profile. I suggest assigning the employee who administers your WordPress website to create the initial version of your LinkedIn company profile page. You need to own the administrative credentials for this profile. However, I recommend that you have your web agency circle back and build out as robust a company profile on LinkedIn as possible. Here are the elements to hold them accountable for delivering:

The advice Bob Misita provided for registering and claiming your profiles with advertising toll collectors applies on LinkedIn as well. The first and most important principle is consistency in the messaging and references back to your website. The roadmap on LinkedIn must be essentially identical to all the other roadmaps to your business on the Internet. However, LinkedIn goes beyond a general profile description, contact information, and a pointer back to your website. It offers a rich feature set for providing specialized media and content.

An example of rich content that LinkedIn presents to visitors is videos that describe your services or highlight customer-success stories. You can repurpose any videos you have produced for your website to display on LinkedIn. Another example of LinkedIn's commitment to your presentation of company value is Slideshare. LinkedIn purchased this online presentation company back in 2012 to enable businesses on LinkedIn to share online slide presentations with potential customers and partners.

The "Recommendations" feature on LinkedIn is similar to the "Reviews" feature on other sites in allowing customers and business partners to endorse you or your business, but it is different because there is no downside risk that they will pan your business with negative feedback. There is no option on LinkedIn to endorse your business for "crappy customer service." LinkedIn also allows you absolute control of the content on your company and product profile pages. There is no filtering on LinkedIn to influence advertising spending.

LinkedIn also allows you to provide updates about your company. For example, if you are sponsoring or participating in a charity golf event, you should definitely post that participation to LinkedIn. Others who are interested might join your cause, and the community you serve will see your involvement and note it as they consider future business for your company.

Just like your website, LinkedIn allows you to generate sublevel "Showcase Pages" for your products. If you have created a brand or specialty message around your services, you may want to build out a Showcase Page highlighting your unique capability. This page should mirror the content you published to your Products and Services page on your website. If you have a standard sales presentation for the product, edit it for any confidential information and post the publically consumable version to your LinkedIn Showcase Page.

Consider all these capabilities and best practices as you provide instructions to your web agency about your expectations for LinkedIn. As they are building out your company profile page, you can begin attaching your employee personal pages to that profile.

Create Employee Profiles

Each of your employees should have a profile on LinkedIn, and it should be consistent, professional, and reflect the standards of your business. Not having a LinkedIn profile is like not having a phone number or an email address.

Start with your own profile and continue to add profiles until all of your employees are featured on LinkedIn. Again, make this easy. Assign a staff member to take photos for profile pictures and write up the profiles for your employees based on their job descriptions. Make certain you customize the URL for each profile, ideally so that the profile link is:

https://www.linkedin.com/in/firstnamelastname

If some of your employees already have LinkedIn profiles, ensure that the information they have about their position with your company is accurate and consistent with your branding.

Encourage your employees to assume control of their profiles as part of their career development. Having profiles on LinkedIn makes it easier for customers to connect with you and your employees so they can recall your business. Search "Billy Marshall" online, and the number two hit after Facebook is my LinkedIn profile. When customers look for you online, you want it to be easy to find you, and your LinkedIn profile can be very helpful in this regard.

Connect to Your Network

As the leader of your business, it is worth your time to be active on LinkedIn at least once a week. The greater your personal network, the more your business opportunities grow.

LinkedIn offers tools for using your email address book and sending connection requests automatically to all of the folks you already know. You can also send manual requests one at a time, but DO NOT SEND RANDOM REQUESTS. If you do not know a person, LinkedIn offers a way to reach out to them through introductions they call "InMail." The more connections you accumulate, the more your profile shows up in searches done by others connected to your network. Your activities directly influence the amount of traffic that passes by your LinkedIn billboard.

Your connections are reflections of your interests and your importance in your area of commerce and expertise. The more connected you become, the easier you are to find. The same applies to your employees, whom you should encourage to build their networks through invitations as well.

As with any powerful online tool, LinkedIn can be misused. If you bomb prospects with unsolicited and irrelevant emails, your company's email domains will be blacklisted as spam domains and your emails will end up in the digital equivalent of the trash can without any review by the customer. Similarly, if you bomb people on LinkedIn with unwelcome and irrelevant connection requests (throwing eggs at the passing traffic from your billboard), you will be blacklisted on that service, too.

Follow All Your Customers

You can have the person in your office who is in charge of your LinkedIn presence log in to your personal profile and "follow" all of your customer companies. Anytime there is any news about these companies, you will get alerts and notifications through LinkedIn. They will also see that you are following them, which makes you more memorable. Your job is to be attentive to your customers, and LinkedIn gives you one more opportunity to do that in a scalable manner using the Internet.

Join Interesting Groups

Although it is not absolutely a requirement, it is a good idea to join groups on LinkedIn that you find interesting or that you believe your customers and prospects will find interesting. Other members of the group will see that you are a member, and perhaps they will connect to you. You will also get notifications about news and discussions promoted by members of the group so you can be responsive and thoughtful when you see notices that impact your customers. Encourage your employees to join groups that reflect their professional interests as well. You will be surprised at the aggregate attention these connections build for your business.

LinkedIn is a key part of your digital wrap, and you do not need to become a social media maven to get benefit from it. Doing the basic work to create profiles for your company, your products and services, yourself, and all of your employees shows high-value customers and partners that you are a serious professional. There are agencies that specialize in using LinkedIn as a lead-generation tool if you wish to invest in advertising on LinkedIn, and I also suggest that you have your web agency help you with your company and product profiles.

Generally speaking, however, most of the work on LinkedIn will be done by you, your appointed administrator, and each of your employees. These connections on LinkedIn are one more element of a digital wrap strategy that makes your business and your expertise more memorable and easier to recall for ongoing service opportunities.

CHAPTER 14

The Digital Wrap Formula for Maximizing the Value of Your Business

At some point you will want to be paid full value for the investment of time, energy, love, and money you have made in your service business. Whether that payday is an arm's-length financial transaction with an unrelated third party, or a passing of the business to the next generation, everyone wants to believe the next owner is receiving something of great value. When your service company becomes more valuable to your customer through implementing the concepts you've read in *The Digital Wrap*, your business is more valuable to the next owner.

The formula for maximizing the value of your service contracting business is pretty simple, but it is amazing how often the formula is ignored amid the chaos of daily operating challenges. Taking some time every month to focus management's attention on the formula and the principles for maximizing value increases your payday when, or if, you decide to cash out.

The formula for valuing a service business is simple:

$$NC * (LVC - CAC) = VALUE$$

NC is the number of customers. Ideally you have many of them because having only a few, even if they are very large, is risky for the future owner; If the new owner loses one or even a few, much of the value of the business is quickly erased.

Business you receive from third parties (manufacturers, management companies, etc.) generally does not count as value. It is too easy for them to unhook you and replace you with someone else because they control the relationship with the customer. Without a direct, persistent, and meaningful connection with the paying customer, your revenue and profit margin are tenuous, and therefore not very valuable to the next owner.

LVC is the lifetime value of a customer. Ideally you get lots of predictable, repeat business from each customer. If each customer is "one and done" with your services, your business is not worth much because you must sustain advertising and sales expenses to promote your brand and attract new customer revenue. As with having only a few customers, the future is risky when the new owner cannot depend on your current customer base for future income streams. As you build your digital wrap, your LVC will increase because you are memorable and easy to recall for more service.

CAC is the cost to acquire a customer. A strong and valuable brand attracts new customers at lower cost because the marketing and sales expense is low when references, customer service, online presence, and brand reputation are strong. Fighting negativity in the market associated with poor customer service and negative reviews is expensive – with a correspondingly high CAC. If you create a wall of negativity due to poor customer satisfaction, your CAC will be much higher. A new owner does not want to spend heavily on advertising to overcome all that market negativity for each new sale.

Your digital wrap is a key value-building strategy because it attracts new customers to your business (increasing NC), maximizes the lifetime value of a customer (increasing LVC), and minimizes the costs of new-customer acquisition (lowering CAC). When your service activities are constantly presented to your customers online, and your service work leaves positive customer impressions all over the Internet, you can build a dominant brand in your service area without heavy expenses for advertising and promotions. Existing customers never leave, and new customers gravitate to your business due to your strong brand, expertise, and hassle-free service capability. Can you imagine an Uber customer ever choosing to use a taxi again when it is so easy to do business with Uber?

Let's do a simple example of this value equation to demonstrate the impact digital wrap principles can have in creating value for your business and wealth for you. Assume you have a business with 5,000 customer locations where you have service contracts, and no single customer has more than 10 to 12 locations (that is, the business is not heavily dependent on any one customer). Assume also that each location delivers an average revenue value of $2,000 per year, and each customer typically stays with your company for 10 years. Further assume that you can demonstrate that you can predictably add 400 new locations each year by spending $200,000 in sales and marketing. With a typical cash contribution margin of 15% for each revenue dollar and a discount value of 15% to bring future cash contributions into today's dollars, the value of the business is $7.45M (see Figure 3) – or .75X the multiple on revenue of $10 million for the business. Remember the Tesla and Ford example? Well, you are better than Ford, which sports a .4X multiple of revenue to value, but you are still trailing far behind Tesla at 18X.

	Base Case	Low Attrition	High Revenue	Low CAC	High Margin
Customer Locations	5,000	5,000	5,000	5,000	5,000
Revenue Per Location	$2,000	$2,000	$2,400	$2,400	$2,400
Total Revenue	$10M	$10M	$12M	$12M	$12M
Lost Locations / Year	500	333	333	333	333
New Locations / Year	400	400	400	600	600
Annual Sales Spending	$200K	$200K	$200K	$200K	$200K
Contribution Margin	15%	15%	15%	15%	18%
Business Value	$7.45M	$8.65M	$10.63M	$12.48M	$15.23M

Figure 3 – Business Valuation Scenarios Table

Now let's assume you can lower your customer attrition so that each customer stays with you for 15 years on average instead of 10 years due to your digital wrap strategy that reminds them of your value and keeps them engaged. The value of your business grows to $8.65M. Because you are gaining more customers than you are losing every year, the business is growing, and it becomes more valuable to the next owner.

If you expand the services you offer (remember artisanal cheese?) and use the knowledge you have of your customer locations to drive email offers and campaigns to increase average revenue value per location from $2,000 to $2,400 per year, the value of your business increases to $10.63M. The business is now at a .9X multiple on the new revenue number of $12 million. No extra sales productivity has been added. You are simply engaging your existing customers more broadly with a broader service line and/ or higher repair revenues associated with data-driven marketing and sales campaigns.

Next assume that all of your service activities on the Internet increase your visibility and reputation in your markets, and you attract 600 new customer locations per year instead of 400 for the same $200,000 in sales and marketing expense. The value of the business increases to $12.48M. This growth comes without expensive marketing campaigns; your growth is driven by higher visibility on the Internet because your digital wrap is constantly visible to your prospects in the digital neighborhood.

Finally, assume you are able to raise prices and enhance your labor productivity with more revenue coming from services that might not require labor or other overhead (monitoring, for example) – increasing your contribution margin from 15% to 18%. Another way to increase margin is to drop the bottom 20% of your customers as you gain confidence in your ability to attract new customers through your online digital wrap capabilities. You can also raise prices as you gain confidence that your customers will stick with you because you are the hassle-free and low-risk provider in the market. Whether it is dropping low-margin customers or raising prices, when you have confidence in your sticking power with your best customers, it is easy to increase overall profit margins.

With all these slight improvements, the same business is now worth \$15.23M – over two times the value of the original scenario. By holding on to your customers 50% longer, expanding your sales to the same customers by just 20%, attracting new customers at a 50% higher rate with similar sales spending, and increasing your contribution margins by just 3%, the value of your business doubled. You do not have to double the size of your business, you simply need to demonstrate that you have a record of increasing sales productivity relative to attrition, expanding sales to existing customers, and increasing margins due to productivity and pricing power. The new owner will happily pay a premium to own a business with a shiny digital wrap for attracting and keeping customers and a well-executed strategy for generating incredible returns on customer wins.

This simple illustration highlights why the digital wrap strategy is critical in creating additional value for your business. Remember these key concepts:

Establish durable, long-lasting connections to customers – The stronger your connection to your customer, the more likely it is to be durable in the face of ever-increasing attention from Internet competitors seeking to unhook you and charge you tolls to reconnect. If you are connecting with your customers online and through frequent reminders of your value, your connections are more memorable, more convenient, and more durable. Customers are constantly reminded of your value, and your relationships with them last forever.

Deliver as many services as you can in which you can claim expertise – The more services you can credibly deliver to your customers, the higher the lifetime value of those customers. You also become more important to them because disconnecting you creates a larger void to fill with a competitor. Do not rely simply on bread and butter, but instead build up a selection of services equivalent to artisanal cheese, tasty snacks, and fine wine (warranties, monitoring, preventative maintenance services).

These items command a premium price and preserve your margins when Internet shopping and price comparison create margin pressure for bread-and-butter services. A broader service portfolio means a longer-lasting connection, higher revenue, and a higher lifetime value for each customer.

Lower your marketing and sales costs – Use your service activities as your online marketing bullhorn. Your digital wrap lets everyone in the digital neighborhood see that you deliver amazing customer service, and it makes you more visible and attractive to new customers who are impressed by your large and loyal following online. Your costs to acquire new customers (CAC) is lower so you can grow faster or trade low-margin customers out of your portfolio for better customers. You have more choices when you have strong demand for your services due to your reputation.

Grow faster – When you use technology to engage your customers, and when some portion of the services you provide requires neither technicians nor administrative manpower (monitoring, warranty, customer self-service), you can grow faster than competitors who are stuck in the mode of adding people and trucks whenever new customers are added. When you replace telephone calls and manual recordkeeping with digital files and online customer engagement, your business grows faster with less capital. Your margins also increase. Computer resources are getting cheaper every day, while labor and steel and fuel will inevitably get more expensive. Computers can work around the clock to serve your customers and deliver your brand value without breaks, benefits, vacations, or sleep. Your customers receive value from your company over and over again without your spending expensive capital for labor and trucks.

Whether your exit strategy is a financial transaction or simply a next-generation succession plan, **committing your business to**

a digital wrap strategy today leads to a better exit outcome in the future. Technology and the Internet are going to change your customers' expectations for what you deliver to them and how you reach them with your value proposition. These changes can be either a going-out-of-business plan or a value-building opportunity. In my opinion, building value is more fun and more rewarding.

CHAPTER 15

Conclusion

I recently gave a talk at a service contracting trade show during which I took my audience through the value-building exercise covered in the last chapter. I began the talk by asking how many in the audience would like to double the value of their business. Of course everyone raised their hand – who wouldn't want their business to be twice as valuable? I then asked them if they had a plan to do that and if they thought it would be easy or fun? No hands. Then I walked them through a few questions to see if they thought some small changes in their businesses were possible.

"How many of you believe you could hold on to each of your customers 50% longer if you showed them what you do for them with email and online service reports? So that customers see what a good job you are doing? So that they trust you because they can see it?" About 60–75% of the audience raised their hand.

"Okay. Do you think you could come up with other services or repairs based on what you observe at their site to increase your revenue from each customer by 20%?" Several folks offered examples of artisanal-cheese upsell ideas, and I saw lots of pen activity in the audience. Most raised their hand indicating they believed that they could indeed raise revenue by 20% at their current customers with some array of artisanal cheese, salty snacks, fine wine, and craft beer service offerings.

"Great. Now how many of you are happy with your online web presence and how it attracts new customers? No one, right? What if I told you that you can use your service activities to post check-ins, reviews, and other relevant information that would rank you number one or two in your area for what you do with zero incremental advertising dollars? Do you think you could double the productivity of your selling and advertising budget if that were true?" Lots of hands in the air. Everyone believed there was room for improvement in the effectiveness of their marketing and sales, and that if they could use service activities to build their site and attract more attention from prospects, that would be great.

"Finally, if you had enough demand potential from new prospects that you felt comfortable dumping the bottom 20% of your customer portfolio, do you believe you could improve your overall margins by 3%?" Once again, all the hands in the room shot up.

"Congratulations," I told them. "You just doubled the value of your business. Did any of that seem hard? Did you have to turn your business upside down?"

The truth is that building a better connection to your customers and taking your service activities online to keep and attract customers is really not that difficult, and it increases the value of your business immensely.

Still skeptical? Consider these examples from ServiceTrade customers:

Karim Nice is the owner and president of Blue Hat Mechanical in Raleigh, North Carolina. At the beginning of 2015, he picked up a 15-location restaurant customer from a competitor. Upon initiating service for the customer, Karim's technicians noticed immediately that much of the equipment was in need of permanent repairs and upgrades due to what Karim describes as a "gas and go" approach used by the former service company. Midway through the first service year, Karim was called to the headquarters office of the customer to explain why the customer was on track to DOUBLE spending on refrigeration and HVAC in 2015.

Karim opened his laptop and projected his ServiceTrade records from their six months of engagement onto the conference room screen. They marched through every online quote record with attached photos and audio descriptions that had been received, reviewed, and approved by the facility managers. "Keep up the good work," the customer relented, "but make certain you always send the evidence behind your repairs so we feel better about spending twice as much with you. Also, we are betting the spending goes down once you get our systems in line. Plan to come back next year and prove it." What an incredible endorsement and display of trust by the customer when presented with the evidence of expertise by the vendor.

Mary Krinbring is the service director at AAA Fire and Safety in Seattle, Washington. She was always a fan of ServiceTrade, but she was very skeptical of my claims that online quotes with photos get approved at a rate three times higher than snail-mail or email with attachments. Mary is not a technology skeptic either, as she began her career with Amazon out in Seattle. She gets it. But 3X the approval rate? Come on, really?

We recently caught up with a phone conversation and she admitted she was wrong and allowed me to crow "I told you so." "We have increased our technician staff by 25% just to cover the volume on the repairs," she admitted to me. "I am so happy that you were right and I was wrong."

Michael Crafton, the CEO at Team 360 Services, has always defined his service company as a technology company. His sales presentations lead with live demonstrations to customers about how 360 collects digital records and represents to the customer the quality of work delivered through online interfaces. His vision of a service company as a technology company has enabled Michael to raise millions of dollars in private capital to acquire and transform companies that were many times the size of his original service business. And these businesses just keep growing as he applies his technology formula to them after acquisition.

These examples illustrate the obvious: Customers want a digital connection to your business. They will pay extra for it. And it doesn't have to be difficult or intimidating. When you connect with them online, you become more valuable to them and, no surprise, your business becomes more valuable, too.

Service contracting is already a great business model with great margins and, historically, few competitive threats. The shifting of labor capacity to low-wage markets overseas that challenged manufacturing companies is not a threat to service contractors because fixing a toilet in Cleveland with labor from China is not possible. The shift of retail purchasing to the Internet that made household names of Amazon and eBay is also not a real threat because services are more complex and not as well-defined or packaged as retail merchandise. The well-established delivery networks of UPS, FedEx and the United States Postal Service that enabled retail to shift to the Internet are not sufficient to deliver skilled labor the same way they deliver packaged merchandise. Uber, however, has certainly demonstrated that local services can be disrupted by technology.

Just as with retail, customers want to see what they are buying and receive information that reinforces their belief that they are receiving a quality product. This information helps them feel wise and comfortable. It eliminates hassles. In retail markets, photos, reviews, and recommendations are examples of information that reinforce a purchasing decision. With Uber, it is a description of the car, the driver, their rating by customers, and how close they are to initiate the pickup. In service contracting, customers want similar comfort regarding their purchases.

Photos, reviews, and recommendations are all good ways to deliver that comfort. Like retail, and as with Uber, customers want updates on the delivery schedule, and these updates need to be proactive and electronic. Different from retail, however, is the expertise and nuance associated with interpreting the technical information that is often associated with skilled trades. Different from retail also is the requirement to have skilled resources on site to perform the service work. Most anyone can drive a car for Uber or deliver a package for Amazon. Not everyone can diagnose and repair a complex piece of equipment.

Technical skills and local resources, however, are simply the table stakes, and there is no premium return for simply playing the table stakes; all players generally meet these minimum requirements. The premium in services comes from a better customer experience – using information, technology, and the Internet to connect with the customer in a way that eliminates risk and hassles. This is the basic formula that Uber has used to build a business valued at $80 billion in just six years.

Building a digital wrap and using the Internet to establish an endearing and enduring connection to your customers helps you command and preserve a premium margin for your services. Don't believe your accounting application provider, however, when they tell you that they have an add-on module that takes care of everything needed for service. Don't confuse the new SaaS and Internet applications with the clunky old PC server applications you purchased five to twenty years ago to manage your back office and accounting operations. Don't believe that any single provider or application will do everything for you either. Do accountants run your customer service department? Do your old applications look like what you see every day on the Internet? The new applications you embrace should make your service and sales activities feel like *amazing service* to the customer. What a great concept! Simply delivering service every day makes you more valuable as a service provider!

Tesla is 40 times more valuable than the typical car company. Some of this premium valuation is due to the growth potential of electric vehicles, but much of it is due to their *direct connection* business model. The manufacturers you represent will follow Tesla's lead, and you need to beat them to the punch by offering an open monitoring solution that covers practically all types of equipment you service. Set the rules of the game before the manufacturer can do it. Instead of taking a 25–30% haircut on your services when the manufacturer offers an extended warranty, you can encourage the customer to *forego* the manufacturer's warranty because you can offer one at a lower cost. You have the data on failure modes and you can monitor the equipment, which makes you a more credible provider of warranty services. The monitoring fees and warranty you sell are the "artisanal cheese" and "fine wine" the customer is craving.

Internet titans, national service companies, and Internet entrepreneurs will be shoving their snouts into your trough to siphon off their share of your high margins. Lead-generation fees, haircuts on revenue when they control the customer, and extortion related to filtering of bad online reviews all represent drags on your business. None of these things are evil in the eyes of the customer. In fact, the customer appreciates the information, scale, and reach provided by these operators. They are an inconvenience to you because they come at your expense. Counter these tactics by posting all the great outcomes you deliver for your customers on your website. Overwhelm the long-distance attempts to connect to your customer with a robust connection of your own. When your customers can retrieve, review, and appreciate your work in digital color all over your website and within their email files, you become invaluable to them. The engagement and impressions you generate with your digital wrap prevent the new competition from ever establishing a connection at all.

The great news is that all of the technology tools of the new competitors are available to you, too. The retail revolution and massive consumer adoption of technology from companies like Apple and Google pave the way for you to have extraordinary capability with minimal expense. All things being equal, the customer will happily choose you to provide services to them at full market price. You just need to make certain all things remain equal by arming yourself with Internet applications and related business practices that give you equivalent or better capability than emerging competitors.

Your digital wrap is the Internet version of your truck wrap, and your services, references, and value proposition create impressions in the digital neighborhood through the simple act of delivering great service. Just like the truck wrap, marketing impressions are a result of service delivery – not an extra or specialized job for someone back in the office to ignore in the daily chaos of managing customer service. Unlike the truck wrap, these digital impressions are not fleeting. They endure forever and build one upon the other until you have an extraordinary platform for launching your sales and marketing activities.

Building a digital wrap is a strategy for creating a more valuable business for you while eliminating many of the daily hassles you experience trying to deliver great customer service. Whether you are planning an exit through a sale or simply by passing the business along to the next generation, learning new tricks and building something valuable is more fun and rewarding than just doing the same old thing every day and worrying about new competitors who are playing by different rules.

Embracing the rules of the Internet is fun because your business becomes differentiated and you get to watch your customers reflect back both the gratitude and the profit that a differentiated service relationship creates. Keeping your customers longer and selling them more services is fun, too. Watching your web presence grow due to your digital wrap without having to become an Internet marketing guru is fun, and it attracts new customers to you just because you are good at what you do. Dropping your aggravating customers because you are confident in the new demand you are creating is fun, and your profits grow as you unload the painful portions of your revenue stream. Using applications to replace the phone-call rodeo between your office, technicians, and customers eliminates hassles for everyone.

The Internet doesn't have to be a drag on your business. The new rules can be fun and rewarding if you are willing to take action. I hope this book gives you the motivation and the confidence to embrace your digital wrap. Go ahead, get out of the truck and go online to own your customers.

About Billy Marshall

Billy is a technology entrepreneur who loves big challenges. He was an early employee at Red Hat, a technology company that has grown from $12 million in sales in 1998 to over $2 billion in 2015. Billy led the Red Hat team that defined the product and sales recipe for "free software." After Red Hat, he founded rPath with a group of Red Hat veterans and helped define the new approach for cloud computing and virtualized applications. ServiceTrade is his current passion because technology can be a significant uplifting force for local and regional service companies – creating good jobs and wealth in the communities they serve.

Local service contracting businesses are currently at risk of being disrupted by Internet entities that will pull the wealth out of communities and leave behind the lowest paying jobs. A college education, with its inflated costs from easy student loans, is often out of reach and increasingly irrelevant for many prospective workers. Strong local service brands can attract, train, and pay good salaries and benefits for a new generation of technology-savvy technicians. Billy founded ServiceTrade to provide a technology path for service contracting companies to build sustainable brands and provide interesting, high-paying jobs for skilled workers.

Billy began his career at General Electric and IBM, and both provided invaluable experience about how to run a high-integrity, customer-focused enterprise. By the grace of God, Billy received an amazing technical education at an incredible price from two storied institutions. He was the recipient of numerous scholarships and financial aid grants at Georgia Tech while becoming the Donnell W. Dutton Most Outstanding Aerospace Senior and the president of Tau Beta Pi, the national engineering honor society. He earned an aerospace engineering degree with highest honors from Georgia Tech. He was also awarded two master's degrees, one in engineering and one in management, from the Massachusetts

Institute of Technology as part of a fellowship program that paid his tuition and expenses in exchange for industry research.

Billy lives in Chapel Hill, North Carolina, with his wife, Jodi, and three lovely daughters, Taylor, Ali, and Carly. When not working to amplify the reach and impact of ServiceTrade, he enjoys offshore fishing and almost every other outdoor sporting activity you can imagine.